The Coming of the Holy Spirit

Mal Couch

The Coming of the Holy Spirit

Copyright © 2001 *by Mal Couch, PhD., Th.D.*

Edited by Johnny Cook

Published by

Tyndale Theological Seminary
Ft. Worth, Texas

in conjunction with
21st Century Press
P.O. Box 8033
Springfield, MO 65801

ISBN 0-9700639-8-9

The cover art is courtesy of the Biblical Arts Center, Dallas, Texas. It is part of a panoramic light and sound presentation of the coming of the Holy Spirit in Acts 2. For more information on the Center, see information in the back of the book.

Cover and book design: Lee Fredrickson: IBIS Design

ABOUT THE AUTHOR

Mal Couch is founder and president of Tyndale Biblical Institute and Seminary in Ft. Worth, TX. He has written several nationally published books.

He has taught full and part-time at such schools as Dallas Seminary, Ouachita Baptist University, Moody Bible Institute and Philadelphia College of the Bible.

He holds a BA. John Brown University; Th.M., Dallas Theological Seminary; MA, Wheaton Graduate School (with honors); Ph.D., Arkansas Biblical Graduate School; Th.D., Louisiana Baptist Theological Seminary.

Dr. Couch has taken 23 trips to the Middle East and Israel. He teaches biblical languages, theology and in depth prophetic studies.

Other books by Mal Couch:
So That's How We Got Our Bible
The Walk Thru The Bible
An Introduction To Classical Evangelical Hermeneutics
A Biblical Theology For The Church
The Fundamentals For The Twenty-First Century
Issues 2000: Evangelical Faith & Cultural Trends In The New Millennium
A Bible Handbook To Acts
Dictionary of Premillennial Theology

DEDICATION

This book is dedicated to Mattie Caruth Byrd. Born of a pioneer Dallas family, Mr. and Mrs. William W. Caruth, Sr., she married the legendary Texas oilman, D. Harold Byrd in 1935.

Among her many accomplishments, she supported the creation of the Miracle at Pentecost painting. The foundation she established provided the land, buildings and sustenance for the Biblical Arts Center which houses the masterpiece.

Mrs. Byrd died in 1972. She did not live to see the completion of the Center, but countless lives have been changed because of her vision.

TABLE OF CONTENTS

CHAPTER 1

A LOOK AT THE TRINITY

Before examining carefully the Doctrine of the Holy Spirit, there needs to be a word about the nature of God Himself and the issue of the Trinity.

The Bible is consistent in its witness as to the nature of God. There is but one God (or One Essence) yet Three Persons (or Personalities) in the Godhead. Though the doctrine of the Trinity (or Triunity of God) is unfathomable, it is one of the most persistent truths of Scripture, running from Genesis to Revelation. The Bible clearly does not proclaim "three" Gods but One:

Hear, O Israel! The Lord is our God, the Lord is one! (Dt. 6:4).

But often God is referred to as "Three-in-One." The Triune God has eternally existed before time and matter was created.

God The Father: *Blessed be the God and Father of our Lord Jesus Christ* (Eph. 1:3).

God The Son: *No man has seen God at any time; the only begotten
                        God who is in the bosom of the Father, He has
                        explained [the Father]* (Jn. 1:18).

                        John the Baptist said, *"And I have seen and have
                        borne witness that this [Jesus] is the Son of God"*
                        (Jo. 1:34).

God The Spirit: Peter said to Ananias, *"In your heart you lied to the
                        Holy Spirit, …You have not lied to men, but to
                        God,"* (Acts 5:34).

                        *Your body is the temple of the Holy Spirit (1 Cor.
                        6:19).*

A. Holy

God is separate from all that is sinful or unclean. There is no evil in God;
He is positively pure and therefore distinct from all others.

"To whom then will you liken Me that I should be his equal?" says the
Holy One (Isa. 40:25).

B. Infinite

God has no boundaries. He is not limited by the universe He created or by
any space-time boundaries. God is everywhere through all periods of time.

*The God who made the world and all things in it, since He is Lord of
heaven and earth, does not dwell in temples made with hands; … He
determined [mankind's'] appointed times, and the boundaries of their
habitation (Acts 17:24-26).*

C. Omniscient

*God knows instantly and effortlessly all matter and all matters, all
minds and every mind, all spirits, every being, all creatures, all plu-
ralities, every law, all relations, all causes, all thoughts, all mysteries,
all enigmas, all feelings, all desires, every unuttered secret, all thrones
and dominions, all personalities, all things visible and invisible in
heaven and in earth, motion, space, time, life, death, good, evil, heav-
en, and hell.*[1]

Declaring the end from the beginning and from ancient times things which have not been done, saying. "My purpose will be established, and I will accomplish all My good pleasure" (Isa. 46:10).

D. Omnipotent

God does all things in line with the truth of His nature. He has no limits unless He chooses to limit Himself for specific reasons. God is called the "Almighty" or "All-Powerful One." Nothing is beyond His capacity to do.

God does according to His will in the host of heaven and among the inhabitants of earth; and no one can ward off His hand or say to Him, "What have you done?" (Dan. 4:35).

E. Omnipresent

God is present everywhere and in everyplace with His entire being.

Where can I go from Your Spirit? Or where can I flee from Your presence? If I should count [Your thoughts to me] they would outnumber the sand [of the sea]. When I awake, I am still with You. (Ps. 139:7, 17-18).

F. Love

In God, love is more than a feeling; it is God's very nature. In God there is no selfishness. He loves the world by providing salvation. He loves His own children by doing them continual good. God's love isn't syrupy for even His discipline reflects His love.

God is love (I Jn. 4:8).

For those whom the Lord loves He disciplines (Heb. 12:6).

Every good thing bestowed and every complete gift is from above, coming down from the Father ... (Ja. 1:17).

G. Eternal

God exists endlessly, forever, and always. God had no beginning and has no ending. There is nothing in God that "runs down." God does not grow nor diminish. He is endlessly self- existent.

From everlasting to everlasting, You are God! (Ps. 90:2).

H. Righteous

Righteousness has to do with God's justice. He is right, fair, moral, and absolute. The Lord can do no wrong. He will always be equitable in His dealings with each human being's situation.

The Lord is righteous (Ps. 11:7).

Righteousness belongs to You, O Lord (Dan. 9:1).

I. Sovereign

God is in absolute control of all that happens in His universe. Concerning God's "permission of sin", it is impossible to reconcile God being sovereign and men being responsible for their own sins. Yet the Bible declares both.

Whatever the Lord pleases, He does, in heaven and in earth, in the seas and in all deeps (Ps. 135:6).

J. Unchanging

God is immutable, never inconsistent. Neither His nature nor His purposes vary. Though active, God is not reactionary as if caught off guard by what man is doing.

For I, the Lord, do not change (Mal. 2:6).

[With God], there is no variation, or shifting shadow (Ja. 1:17).

K. The Holy Spirit Shares The Attributes Of God

Since the Holy Spirit is Deity, He shares the attributes that characterize God.

Holiness	*The Comforter, the Holy Spirit, which the Father will send in My name, He shall teach you all things,* (John 14:26).
Infinite	(Infinity defined as no bounds or limits.) *Where can I go from Your Spirit?* (Ps. 139:7).
Omniscient	*The things of God know no one but the Spirit of God,* (I Cor. 2:10-11).

Omnipotent	*The Spirit moved across the waters [in creation],* (Gen. 1:2).
Omnipresent	*Where shall I go from Your Spirit? Or where shall I flee from Your presence?* (Ps. 139:7-8)
Love	*The grace of the Lord Jesus Christ, and the love of God, and the communion (sharing) of the Holy Spirit be with you all,* (II Cor. 13:14).
Eternal	*The blood of Christ who through the eternal Spirit offered Himself,* (Heb. 9:14).
Righteous	*Through the Spirit we wait for righteousness, with anticipation!* (Gal. 5:5).
Sovereign	*The Spirit works all these things, ... just as He wills,* (I Cor. 12:11).

The divinity of the Holy Spirit is so clearly revealed in Scripture that very few have dared to call it in question. ... Christ uses the pronouns, I, you, he, when speaking of the relation of the Holy Spirit to himself and the Father: "I will send him." "He will testify of me." "Whom the Father will send in my name." Thus he is sent; he testifies, he takes of the things of Christ, and shows them to us. He teaches and leads to all truth. He knows, because he searches the deep things of God. ...

The New Testament throughout all its teachings discovers the plan of redemption as essentially involving the agency of the Holy Spirit in applying the salvation which it was the work of the Son to accomplish. The Spirit inspired the prophets and apostles; he teaches and sanctifies the church; he selects her officers, qualifying them by the communication of special gifts at his will. He is the advocate, every Christian is [in his care]. He brings oil the grace of... Christ to us, and gives its affect to us in every moment of our lives.[2]

L. Personality And The Spirit

As mentioned, the Bible pictures the Spirit as a person, with characteristics of personality. The Spirit inspires, resides, knows relationally, and may be moved emotionally. Below is a list that describes this aspect of the Spirit of God:

1. The Spirit is said to have a mind. *"The mind of the Spirit"* (Rom. 8:27). Mind is an attribute of personality.

2. The Spirit makes intercession for believers. *"The Spirit intercedes for the saints,"* (Rom. 8:27). As well, Christ intercedes for believers, (I John 2:1-2).

3. The Spirit is pictured as "personality." He may be grieved (Eph. 4:30); insulted (Heb. 10:29); lied to (Acts 5:3); blasphemed and sinned against (Matt. 12:31-32).

4. As God, the Spirit can be known. *"You know Him (the Spirit) because He abides with you, and will be in you"* (John 14:17).

5. As God, the Spirit speaks truth. *"The Spirit of truth"* (John 14:17).

6. As God, the Spirit inspired the Scriptures. *"Holy men of God spake as they were moved by the Holy Spirit"* (I Pet. 1:21).

7. The Spirit gives us access to God the Father. *"Through Him (Jesus Christ) we have access by One Spirit unto the Father"* (Jude 20-21).

CHAPTER 2

INTRODUCTIONS

Confusion reigns on issues of the Holy Spirit. Though the verses we have looked at are clear in regard to the Holy Spirit, most Christians are not reading their Bibles. Therefore, today there is mass confusion about the Doctrine of the Holy Spirit. Many are asking: Is the Spirit a person? Is it (or he?) simply a power or force? Is the Spirit of God some kind of glue that holds the universe together? Is He indeed personality and deity?

And more especially, how does He work today with believers? Is He passive or is He directing all affairs that swirl around the individual Christian? Too, does He dwell within? Can He ever leave the believer? How does He cause change in the child of God?

Today there is a great de-emphasis of strong Bible teaching and personal Bible study. Because of this people know little about major doctrines. This particularly applies to the Doctrine of the Holy Spirit.

Surprisingly, Christians often go from one extreme to another in attempting to explain the Holy Spirit. Some see Him simply as an outside force and an influence that really cannot be explained. Others believe that feelings and emotional excitement are evidence that the Holy Spirit is at work.

But what is the biblical balance and what is the truth about God's Spirit?

15

A. The Spirit And The New Age

The world, of course, is really confused about the Holy Spirit, because it does not see the Bible as an authoritative source of knowledge about any divine truth. Part of the problem lies with the fact that we are in the period of the cult of the New Age. The New Age is a combination of Pantheism, Humanism and a revival of Hinduism that is now penetrating into Western thinking. The New Age generally presents the idea of the Spirit as the great power or force.

Without question, the average person who is unchurched and unfamiliar with the Word of God thinks of the Holy Spirit in New Age terminology. New Age writer Bill Cane pictures all of mankind and the world in Pantheistic light. He see all peoples and religions joining hands and unified by the "Spirit of peoples" who in turn see the world as the great Mama.

New Agers talk about the spirit of solidarity and the spirit and energy that draws all peoples into a communion. Cane says:

> *"Spend time with a flower, among the trees, at the park. The womb of Gaia (the Mother spirit force of the world) can nourish us, heal us and give us new life, if we let her."*[3]

Ancient cultures had a concept of the Spirit of God often simply called the Great Spirit. Of course this belief echoes back to the early accounts of Genesis whereby the Spirit of God is active in the creation of the world and also in judging the sinfulness of men just before the Flood. Almost all religious cultures reflect the true stories found in the early biblical accounts.

The Stoney Indians of Canada experience a misguided view of the Spirit this way:

> *"We were on pretty good terms with the Great Spirit, creator and ruler of all. We saw the Great Spirit's work in almost everything: sun, moon, trees, ... sometimes we approached him [the Great Spirit] through these things."*[4]

This distorted, limited, and untruthful notion of the Spirit of God is what dominates other religious cultures. Unfortunately, this eclectic teaching about the Spirit of God is what is prevalent today.

This book intends to examine carefully the biblical record and revelation of the Holy Spirit. Without a firm understanding of Him and His work, the believer is limited in terms of his Christian growth and spiritual experience.

This book hopes to deal with the following questions:

1. How has the Spirit of God operated in the various Dispensations and Ages of the past?

2. What does the Holy Spirit have to do with the Christian walk and experience?

3. Does the Holy Spirit produce ascetic or mystical experiences within the believer?

4. How does the Holy Spirit produce fruit and maturity in the life of the child of God? Is the Filling of the Spirit simply for emotional show? Is an emotional experience the most important work of the Holy Spirit?

What are the purposes of the gifts of the Holy Spirit? Are they for *show* or, in a very pragmatic sense, helpful in dramatically witnessing through the body of Christ? And, are the gifts of the Holy Spirit (especially the gift of linguistics) simply for making believers feel good?

B. Importance Of This Study

The Holy Spirit comes under the general area of Theology called Pneumatology. This field of Systematics deals with all biblically revealed facts concerning the Holy Spirit. Today there is much talk about the third person in the Trinity but little true scriptural knowledge.

On Pneumatology, Chafer notes:

Pneumatology is the scientific treatment of any or all facts related to [S]pirit. ... Whatever is true of the triune God is true of the Holy Spirit. This averment may be made with equal justification of the Father or the Son, and, if heeded in regard to the Third Person, will go far toward the right understanding and estimation of the Person and work of the Holy Spirit.... Constructive teaching [on the Holy Spirit] is needed, and pastors and teachers would do well to measure the amount of emphasis that should be given to this theme in accord with the extent to which it appears in the New Testament text, rather than to fall into and become party to the prevailing neglect of these portions of vital truth.[5]

On the importance of the study, Dr. A.A. Hodge writes:

> *The divinity of the Holy [Spirit] is so clearly revealed in Scripture that*
> *very few have dared to call it in question. ... The New Testament*
> *throughout all its teachings discovers the plan of redemption as essen-*
> *tially involving the agency of the Holy Ghost in applying the salvation*
> *which it was the work of the Son to accomplish. He inspired the*
> *prophets and apostles; he teaches and sanctifies the church: he selects*
> *her officers, qualifying them by the communication of special gifts at*
> *his will. ... He brings all the grace of the absent Christ to us, and gives*
> *it effect in our persons in every moment of our lives.*[6]

Finally Enns concludes:

> *Because the Holy Spirit is a member of the triune Godhead the special*
> *study of His person and work could not be more important. As might*
> *be expected wherever God and His truth are involved, false teaching*
> *has developed to distort or deny orthodox doctrine. The Bible is rich*
> *with data about the Spirit from which a major theological segment*
> *can be readily constructed.*[7]

C. How To Approach This Study

In trying to understand the Biblical doctrine of the Holy Spirit, this study will have as its main point of reference the Word of God. Using a normal, customary, and literal approach to hermeneutics, we will come to the Word of God and let it speak to us. We will not impose human emotional experience to determine doctrine. The written record in the revelation of our Bible is sufficient to determine what the Lord has to say on the subject. Some try to use extra evidence in attempting to figure out how the Spirit of God works but subjective experience varies from person to person and is not determinative in creating a truth that all can agree upon. Only by looking carefully in the Hebrew and Greek texts, and at context, can we know revelation in regard to the Holy Spirit.

D. The Names Of The Holy Spirit

Very often in Scripture we simply have the expression "The Spirit of God" or "The Spirit." There are references also to "The Spirit from Christ." In both Old and New Testament "Holy Spirit" means the same thing. The Hebrew word (*Kodesh*) means holy or that which is separate, unique, and special. The same definition would apply to the New Testament

Greek word (*Hagios*). The Hebrew word (*Ruach*) and the Greek word (*Pneumatos*) both mean spirit or wind. This term was given to describe the Holy Spirit because He is unseen. Too, He is unfelt and moves among men as a wind that cannot be seen or touched.

The Spirit is the third person of the Trinity. He has the characteristics of personality and He is very Deity. He is not simply an influence, abstract energy, or power. The Spirit has all the attributes of God in terms of eternality, holiness and all the other characteristics found revealed about the Lord Himself. It is the error of the Pagan and New Age religions to simply see the Spirit as a force. Of course, that concept is a distortion of the original biblical revelation. False philosophies and false religions are but half-truths that distort or deprecate God's clear revelation found only in the Bible.

E. The Deity Of The Holy Spirit

The Holy Spirit is very God. Generally the masculine pronoun He is used when referring to the Spirit. All the attributes of God are used to describe the Holy Spirit. But as well, almost all the works of God the Father and of the Son are applied to Him.

When Christians think about the Spirit of God, they must stand in awe to realize that they are not simply dealing with some abstract force. But they are referring to the divine Person who dwells within, who takes up residence, and who influences and controls the behavior of the believer.

From the Old to the New Testaments the Bible is consistent as to how it describes the Spirit of God. He is seen in the first few verses of Genesis as one of the initiators of creation and life on earth, including mankind. And yet the Spirit of God is not part of creation as is taught in pantheism. Pantheism sees matter, man, and the animal world all intertwined with god or the spirit of god. In other words, we are god (or gods) ourselves, as is all things. And everything is part of "spirit."

The New Agers speak of this concept of the unity of the spirit that holds or binds all things together. But the Bible sees matter as completely separate from God Himself. Matter is separate from the work of the Holy Spirit. And yet the Spirit of God is everywhere. He influences, controls, and changes situations.

As mentioned, He is a separate personality from God the Father and God the Son. And yet the three persons in the Godhead are still but one God. This mystery of the Trinity is unfathomable but crucial to Divine revelation from the first to the last books of our Scriptures.

The great Christian writer Arthur Pink puts it this way:

> *[We will] show from the Word of Truth that the Holy Spirit is distinguished by such names and attributes, that He is endowed with such a plentitude of underived power, and that He is the Author of such works as to altogether transcend finite ability, and such as can belong to none but God Himself.*[8]

Smeaton also helps explain the Holy Spirit when he writes:

> *Wherever Christianity has become a living power, the doctrine of the Holy Spirit has uniformly been regarded, equally with the atonement and justification by faith, as the article of a standing or falling Church. The distinctive feature of Christianity, as it addresses itself to man's experience is the work of the Spirit, which not only elevates it far above all philosophical speculation, but also above every other form of religion.*[9]

Pache well concludes when he notes:

> *The unity of the three Persons of the Trinity does not prevent Them from each playing a particular part. The Father is greater than all (John 10:29). The Son does only what He sees the Father doing and fulfills His will (John 5:19, 30). The Holy Spirit is sent by the Father and by the Son (John 14:26 and 16:7); He is given in answer to the prayer of the Son and in His name; and His role is to glorify the Son by putting His presence in the hearts of His disciples. (John 14:16, 26 and 16:14).*
>
> *On the other hand, the unity between the Son and the Spirit is marked by the fact that the attitude adopted by men toward the one determines that which they maintain toward the other: he who rejects Christ resists the Holy Spirit; the one who accepts the Savior receives the Holy Spirit; he who yields entirely to Jesus is used by the Holy Spirit.*[10]

F. The Holy Spirit And The Inspiration Of The Old Testament

The very word "inspire" implies the "breathing" work of God's Spirit. The main passage on the doctrine of Inspiration is II Timothy 3:16-17:

All Scripture is inspired by God and profitable for teaching, for reproof for correction, for training in righteousness; that the man of God may be adequate, equipped for every good work.

"Inspired" is actually two words put together:

Theos = God, and Pneustos = spirit or breath. Many believe this is really saying more than "God-breathed," but instead: God's - Spirit! "All Scripture comes by God's Spirit." There would be indicators for this as we study various passages on the subject.

Without doubt, the Bible claims the Holy Spirit as the Divine author of Scripture!

We read:

For no prophecy was ever made by an act of human will, but men moved by the Holy Spirit spoke from God (II Peter 1:21).

The Scriptures had to be fulfilled, which the Holy Spirit foretold by the mouth of David ... [Psalm 41:9 is quoted], (Acts 1:16).

The Holy Spirit rightly spoke through Isaiah the prophet to your fathers, saying [Isaiah 6:9 is quoted], (Acts 28:25b).

Just as the Holy Spirit says [Psalm 95:7 is quoted], (Heb. 3:7).

The Holy Spirit is signifying this [Leviticus 16:12-on is referred to], (Heb. 9:8).

And the Holy Spirit also bears witness to us ... [Jeremiah 31:33-34 is quoted], (Heb. 10:15-17).

CHAPTER 3

THE HOLY SPIRIT IN THE OLD TESTAMENT

A. The Spirit In Creation

Right up front in the beginning of the Bible, the Holy Spirit is mentioned as having a key role in creation. *"The Spirit of God was hovering (moving, vibrating, fluttering gently) over the surface of the waters"* (Gen. 1:2). As revelation progresses in Scripture, it is clear the Spirit is not simply a force, but an intelligent personality that creates, responds, and moves with definite determination.

On Genesis 1:2 Morris writes:

> *The word "Spirit" is the Hebrew (ruach), which is also the word for "wind" and "breath." The context determines which is the correct meaning in any given instance. In Genesis 1:2, there is no doubt that the creative activity requires not a wind but the person of God Himself Since the universe was everywhere in need of activation, that person of the Godhead who is both omnipresent and energizing is appropriately mentioned as working in the creation at this point.*

This activity of the Holy Spirit is called that of "moving" in the presence of the waters. The word "moved" (Hebrew rachaph) occurs only three times in the Old Testament, the other two being translated "shake" (Jeremiah 23:9) and "fluttereth" (Deuteronomy 32:11), respectively. Some commentators relate the word particularly to the hovering of a mother hen over her chicks. In any case, the idea seems to be mainly that of a rapid back and forth motion.

In modern scientific terminology, the best translation would probably be "vibrated." If the universe is to be energized, there must be an Energizer. If it is to be set in motion, there must be a Prime Mover.[11]

B. The Holy Spirit Strives With Sinful Mankind

The Spirit is not mentioned again until the Dispensation of Conscience. The great worldwide flood would end the period of Conscience. This period of early history would fail because, as the Lord looks at evil and fallen humanity, He is "moved to grief" and "deeply pained" at what He sees (Gen. 6:6). The Lord adds, *"My Spirit will not strive (execute a vindication) forever with man ... (6:3).* Obviously, during this age of early development, man was spiraling deeper into the abyss of sin. A limit would be reached in the Spirit's convicting work against evil.

Morris adds:

As the moral and spiritual character of the antediluvian world degenerated, ... it was apparent that the people had become so hopelessly corrupt as to be beyond reclamation. They had completely and irrevocably resisted the Spirit's witness, so that it was futile any longer for Him to "strive" with man. This word (Hebrew doon) is used only here and is therefore of somewhat uncertain meaning, possibly including also the idea of "judging."

Since the witness of God's Spirit to man's spirit had been rejected, there was no purpose to be served any longer in maintaining his physical life and continued multiplication. There may also be an implicit suggestion that man had become no better than animals: ...

This antediluvian witness of the Holy Spirit to man must have been accomplished by the preaching of God's Word through one of His prophets. It is known that both Enoch and Noah bore a strong witness to the people of their day, and it is possible that Methuselah and Lamech did the same.[12]

Leupold sums up:

> *In spite of all the Spirit's corrective efforts "mankind" ('adham) had persisted in abandoning the way of truth and life. Men had finally, as the one suggestive illustration showed, no longer cared about having their homes centers of godly instruction where divine truth prevailed, being taught by father and by mother, but instead chose any woman whatsoever, as the fang of the moment moved them, to rear their offspring. At that point God determines that He will let His Spirit no longer do His work of reproving and restraining (yadhon), because man has degenerated. Man is no longer simply sinful, as he has been right along since the Fall; the race has also as a whole practically sunk to the level of being "flesh" (basar), just plain, ordinary, weak and sinful stock, abandoned to a life of sin. Man has forfeited all hope of further efforts of God's grace.[13]*

C. The Spirit Of God Giving Us Life

Genesis was compiled and composed by Moses, under the inspiration of the Holy Spirit, probably during the Wilderness Wandering: 1445-1405 BC. Genesis records the very beginning of all things, starting with eternity past. Our oldest Old Testament book is Job, written probably about 2,000 B.C.

Though Job has only two references concerning the Spirit, the following powerful and awesome statement is given by inspiration through Elihu: *"The Spirit of God has made me, and the breath of the Almighty gives me life"* (33:4). With great boldness, Elihu tells us that if it were not for the Lord's Spirit sustaining life, all that lives would instantly perish! *"If [God] should gather to Himself His Spirit and His breath, all flesh would perish together, and man would return to dust"* (34:14-15).

Keil & Delitzsch note:

> *For the life of the animal is only the individualizing of the breath of the Divine Spirit. The spirit of man on the contrary, is an inspiration directly coming forth from God the personal being, transferred into the bodily frame, and therefore forming a person. [Man thus stands] in the exalted consciousness of having been originated by the Spirit of God, and being endowed with life from the inbreathed breath of the Almighty...[14]*

D. The Holy Spirit Working In Joseph

In the story of Joseph in Egypt, Pharaoh notes the extraordinary moral character and spiritual depth of this young man. When Joseph was put in charge of the entire food supply of the nation, his proposal to ration all the grain reserves pleased Pharaoh "and all his servants" (Gen. 41:37). Then Pharaoh asks: *"Can we find a man like this, in whom is a divine Spirit?"* (Gen. 41:38). Leupold comments:

> *The thought that stands out in reference to Joseph is that he has "God's Spirit." The Egyptians still had so much spiritual discernment as to be able to see that a supernatural element had been involved in this interpretation.*[15]

And Morris adds to this thought:

> [The Egyptians] also recognized that [Joseph] was a man of unique spiritual attributes and that, indeed, this was the real reason for his other abilities. Though they could hardly have understood the doctrine of the Holy Spirit and the filling of the Spirit, nevertheless they acknowledged that in Joseph dwelt the Spirit of God (Hebrew *ruach elohim*). He had indeed *"professed a good profession before many witnesses"* (I Timothy 6:12). [16]

Actually, the Hebrew text of 41:38 reads "Spirit of Elohim." Some Bible versions use the word "divine" because biblical scholars have trouble believing Pharaoh could refer to the Spirit of the One God of the Universe! But we now know that the remembrance of the God of Scripture lingered for generations from the point of the Garden of Eden and the Fall of Adam! Though polytheism was crowding out the truth, many still had the recall of that which was genuine!

The Holy Spirit was clearly working through Joseph and giving him wisdom and spiritual insights. Pharaoh, though a pagan, recognized this fact.

E. The Spirit Of God In The Designers Of The Tabernacle

During the Dispensation of Law, the Spirit did not indwell all believers. But He came into godly men for specific tasks. In building the Tabernacle, the Holy Spirit filled Bezalel, the son of Uri, with wisdom, understanding and knowledge in all kinds of craftsmanship (Ex. 31:2-3). As well, the Lord, more than likely by His Spirit, put skill into the hearts of others so they could fashion garments, utensils and furniture "according to all that I have commanded" (Ex. 31:6-11). This was not a permanent filling or indwelling but was temporary in order to accomplish a spiritual task.

F. The Spirit Giving Discernment To The Elders

The Spirit of the Lord was working within Moses in order that he too would know the mind of God in leading the children of Israel in the wilderness wandering. But because of the crush of problems Moses faced, seventy elders were appointed to help him. God "took" His Spirit that was "upon" Moses and placed Him upon these men so that they as well would have ability to help guide this mob of Jews who were moving through the desert (Num. 11:17-29). As the Spirit rested upon the elders, they were able to prophecy only "once" but never again (11:25). The sign was given but one time, showing that God's Spirit was working now also with them.

As Moses came to the end of his blessed and fruitful life, he laid hands upon Joshua as a sign to the nation that the leadership and responsibility were passed on to him. Then, Joshua as well was "filled" with the Spirit of wisdom (Dt. 34:9). Though some see "spirit" in the passage in lower case, and simply as an attitude or influence, more than likely this was indeed the Spirit of God!

G. The Judges Indwelt By God's Spirit

The Holy Spirit indwelt four of the judges in the book of Judges. Other judges as well may have also been so controlled but the Scriptures fail to mention it. Othniel, Gideon, Jephthah, and Samson are the ones upon whom the Spirit fell. Of Samson, the text says he was "stirred" by the Spirit from the Lord. (Ju. 13:25). And, the Holy Spirit came upon him "mightily" to grant extra physical strength and ability when confronted with the Philistines who wished to kill him (14:6, 19; 15:14).

H. The Holy Spirit Working With King Saul

King Saul is an enigma in the Old Testament. Because his actions were so erratic and unpredictable, some do not believe he was ever a child of God. But it would be difficult to think that the Holy Spirit would come within him if he did not belong to the Lord as His own! Yet the violent ups and downs of this man are indeed strange.

Samuel foretold that the Spirit of the Lord would mightily come upon him and Saul would prophesy and *"be changed into another man"* (I Sam.

10:6). The Holy Spirit apparently often came and went, in terms of His use and control of Saul. Sometimes Saul prophesied, sometimes he became angry against sin because of the influence of the Spirit (10:10; 11:6).

But in time, because of Saul's rebellion, the "Spirit of the Lord departed from Saul, and an evil spirit from the Lord terrorized him" (16:14). For His sovereign purposes God may manipulate and use the demonic spirits as He pleases. They can act as a scourge from the Lord to judge the person involved or drive that individual back to God.

I. The Special Work Of The Spirit In David

King David was used of the Lord as a prophet. As David rehearsed his life toward the end, he realized this special privilege given to him by the Lord. *"The Spirit of the Lord spoke by me, and His word was on my tongue"* (II Sam. 23:2).

Luke, the author of Acts, picks up on this and records that the Holy Spirit spoke through the mouth of *"our father David Your servant ..."* (Acts 4:25). Luke particularly points to Psalm 2 as penned by David but he clearly, as an instrument in the hands of God, prophesied by the power of the Spirit: *"The rulers were gathered together against the Lord, and against His Christ"* (4:26).

Often, David wrote about the Holy Spirit. He pleaded with God not to remove His Spirit after his sin with Bathsheba: *"Do not cast me away from Your presence, and do not take Your Holy Spirit from me"* (Ps. 51:11). This does not imply a loss of salvation for David but it tells us David feared the Lord would no longer be using him as before.

J. The Spirit Gives Life And Takes Away Life

As Elihu had said in the book of Job, it is God's Spirit that sustains life, indeed, that actually creates life in an ongoing process of generation. In other words, the continual creation of life is not automatic; the Holy Spirit renews it constantly. *"[All created life] wait(s) for You, to give them their food in due season. ... You send forth Your Spirit, they are created; and You do renew the face of the ground"* (Ps. 104:27-30).

Kirkpatrick has this to say on this passage:

> *May this manifestation of God in Nature ever continue! May Jehovah never cease to rejoice in His works as He rejoiced when He pronounced all things to be very good [in the beginning]* (Gen. 1:31; Prov. 7:31). *A*

look, a touch are enough to remind the earth of the awful power of its Creator, Who if He willed could annihilate as easily as He created.

But life not death rules in Nature. A new generation takes the place of the old. Creation continues, for God is perpetually sending forth His [S]pirit, and renewing the face of the earth with fresh life.[17]

Keil & Delitzsch add as well:

The existence, passing away, and origin of all beings is conditioned by God. His hand provides everything; the turning of His countenance towards them upholds everything; and His breath, the creative breath, animates and renews all things. The spirit of life of every creature is the disposing of the divine Spirit, which hovered over the primordial waters and transformed the chaos into the cosmos.[18]

K. The Holy Spirit Of God Is Everywhere!

David further makes it clear that God's Spirit is omnipresent or everywhere. He further notes that God and His Spirit are the same! *"Where can I go from Your Spirit? Or where can I flee from Your presence?"* (Ps. 139:7). Note the parallelism. *"How can I go from Your Spirit ... flee from Your presence?"* God is omnipresent! The Spirit is omnipresent!

God, however, is omnipresent, sustaining the life of all things by His Spirit, and revealing Himself either in love or in wrath ...[19]

L. The Spirit Coming Upon The Future Messiah

As the Old Testament unfolds by the process of Progressive Revelation, the prophecy of the coming of an Anointed One (Messiah) grows from prophet to prophet. Isaiah calls Him the Shoot, the Branch who will come forth from the root of Jesse, or through David and his father (Isa. 11:1). *"And the Spirit of the Lord will rest on [this Branch]"* (11:2). Isaiah says this is the Spirit of wisdom, understanding, counsel, strength, knowledge, and fear of the Lord (11:2). By this the prophet sees this Anointed One as human but totally controlled in His thoughts and actions by the Holy Spirit.

In the coming Dispensation of the Kingdom and the Millennial reign the Messiah, this Branch of David will completely delight in the Lord; He will not judge by human principles but will legislate with divine righteous standards (11:3-4). Isaiah implies His rule is worldwide because in judgment He

strikes the earth with the scepter of His words and, He decides fairly for
the afflicted of the world (11:4).

Isaiah then pictures during the Dispensation of the Kingdom a world of
near perfect peace. The wild animals will be contained (11:6). *"The leopard
will lie down with the kid." "The lion will eat straw."* And, *"the earth will be
full of the knowledge of the Lord as the waters cover the sea"* (11:9).

The entire world will pay respect to the Messiah, the Anointed, and the
root of Jesse!

*"The nations will resort to the root of Jesse, who will stand as a [flag] for
the [earth's] peoples; and [the Messiah's] resting place will be glorious"*
(11:10). And it is the Holy Spirit who mysteriously works within the
Messiah Jesus to grant understanding, strength and knowledge!

M. The Providential Work Of The Spirit In Others
The nations of Judah and Israel had years earlier turned their backs
against Jehovah. In 722 B.C., the Northern nation, Israel, was led away to
Assyria. In 586 B.C., the great Temple in Jerusalem was destroyed and
thousands of Jews were deported to Babylon.

With this as background, Isaiah along with Ezekiel, speaks more of the
Spirit of the Lord than the other prophets all together, though the other
seers and the minor prophets of the Lord have much revelation to give us
about God's Spirit as well.

But for example, just before exile, Isaiah castigates the Southern
Kingdom of Judah for considering making an ungodly alliance with Egypt.
The Lord has him write: *"Woe to [you] rebellious children ... who execute a
plan, but [it is] not Mine, and [you who] make an alliance [with Egypt], but
not by My Spirit, in order to add sin to sin; ... without consulting Me, to take
refuge in the safety of Pharaoh..."* (30:1-2). God makes it clear that it was not
the Holy Spirit who inspired this defensive agreement. The Lord's Spirit
was available to give guidance and grant wisdom to Judah's leadership but
they spurned His influence.

N. The Spirit And Future Restoration
As Isaiah distresses over the sins of Israel, God gives him a vision of
restoration that will someday be fulfilled in the coming Dispensation of the
future Kingdom. That restoration will be inspired by the Holy Spirit
through what is elsewhere called the New Covenant. Isaiah writes of judgment: The land full of briars and thorns. The palace of the king abandoned.
The cities forsaken ...

"Until the Spirit is poured out upon us from on high, and the wilderness becomes a fertile field and the fertile field is considered a forest [Then] the work of righteousness will be peace forever. Then my people will live in a peaceful habitation..." (32:15-17).

O. The Holy Spirit Working In Israel's New Birth

Speaking to a future generation of Jews, Ezekiel predicts the conversion of Israel when God's Spirit brings about a new birth:

"I will give you a new heart and put a new spirit within you; ... I will put My Spirit within you and cause you to walk in My statutes, ... and you will live in the land that I gave to your forefathers; so you will be My people, and I will be your God" (36:26-28).

"I will put My Spirit within you, and you will come to life, and I will place you on your own land." "'I will not hide My face from them any longer, for I shall have poured out My Spirit on the house of Israel,' declares the Lord God." (37:14; 39:29).

The prophet Joel (cir. 835 B.C.) picks up on this prophecy of the Spirit someday being poured forth. Yet God gave him the vision that it will be upon "all mankind" as well as upon Israel, (2:28-29). (But more on this New Covenant, its fulfillment with Israel and the Gentiles, and the work of the Holy Spirit, in a later chapter.)

P. The Personality And Emotions Of God's Spirit

In a judgment section of the prophetic book of Micah (cir. 700 B.C.), the emotions and personality of the Spirit are again made clear. In the context, some felt God was too harsh in His condemnation of sin: *"Is the Spirit of the Lord impatient? Are these [judgments] His doings?"* (2:7). Notice that the Spirit can be emotionally impatient (or angry), and the judgments are His initiative, Note also that the masculine possessive pronoun "His" is used.

Again, the Spirit of God is not simply a force or power but He is personality!

Micah lets his readers know that his words are not simply the expression of his own mind. He references the fact that in his day there was an army of false diviners, seers and misleading prophets who led the people astray (3:5-7). These men would bring spiritual darkness upon the people as if the sun was setting and the day was becoming as blackness all around them (3:6).

Q. The Spirit's Inspiration Of The Prophets

But Micah knew the Holy Spirit was inspiring his words as a prophet of God. He penned:

"On the other hand I am filled with power with the Spirit of the Lord and with justice and courage to make known to Jacob his rebellious act, even to Israel his sin" (3:8).

The phrase "to make known" tells us how and why God inspired the true prophets to speak to His people. They were voices motivated and directed by the Holy Spirit to vocalize the truth.

The ministry of the prophet Haggai (around 520 B.C.) was to rebuke the exiles that were returning from Babylon to Jerusalem. Because of fear they were delaying the rebuilding of the Temple. Haggai encouraged them to set to work.

Through Haggai the Lord spoke words of encouragement to Zerubbabel, Joshua the son of Jehozakak, the high priest, and all the people of the land. God said, *"I am with you ... My Spirit is abiding in your midst; do not fear!"* (2:5). God the Father was there and His Spirit as well! They provided direction and guidance to the rebuilding of the Temple and the city of Jerusalem.

R. The Spirit Working In The Returning Jews

During the period of the reconstruction of the great Temple, the prophet Zechariah (cir. 520 B.C.) was active in a spiritual leadership role along with Haggai and Zerubbabel. Through Zechariah, and to Zerubbabel, the Lord gives this famous promise:

"'Not by might nor by power, but by My Spirit,' says the Lord of Hosts" (Zech. 4:6).

The Lord was reminding Zerubbabel (who had a tremendous organizational and leadership role) that He had His purposes for Israel, the Jews and the land, that would not be thwarted! His Spirit would accomplish what Jehovah wished!

In Zechariah, in an encounter similar to Jesus' spiritual and physical testing in the wilderness (Matthew 4), Satan accuses the high priest

Joshua. But the Lord answers in Zechariah 3:2: *"The Lord rebuke you, Satan! Indeed, the Lord who has chosen Jerusalem rebuke you! Is this not a brand plucked from the fire?"* (A reference to the fact that the people have returned from the "furnace" of captivity.)

All that God wants to do with this returning generation; He will do through the operation of His Holy Spirit! His Spirit will carry out the Lord's sovereign purpose and decree for the returnees!

S. Conclusion

The Old Testament is rich and full in its teaching on the Holy Spirit. Below is a list of what we have discovered so far:

1. The Holy Spirit played a role in preparing earth for the creation of life (Gen. 1:2).

2. The Holy Spirit is not simply an inanimate force but is personality who can "judge" or strive with sinful man (Gen. 6:3).

3. The Holy Spirit is directly involved in the creation of each of us individually (Job 33:4).

4. When the Spirit withdraws, all living things including man, die (Job 34:14-15). As well, the Spirit creates new life over and over again (Ps. 104:27-30).

5. The Spirit came upon specific men in giving direction and wisdom in the building of the Tabernacle (Es. 31:2-3; 6-11).

6. The Spirit imparted wisdom and godliness in men such as Joseph (Gen. 41:38).

7. The Spirit rested upon key prophets such as Moses, David, and many others. He also fell upon the elders Moses appointed to help him govern (Num. 11:17-29).

8. The Spirit rested upon the judges God used to rule the people after they had entered the land (Ju. 13:25).

9. The Spirit is everywhere, or omnipresent just as Jehovah (Ps. 139:7).

10. The Spirit would rest upon the coming Branch or Messiah; He would give to Him divine wisdom for obeying the Lord (Isa. 11:1-4).

11. In a broad sense, the Spirit convicted the leaders of Israel in regard to God's will or desire on certain matters. Often, they would not heed this conviction (Isa. 30:1-2).

12. In the future Kingdom restoration, the Holy Spirit will cause the Jews to be "born again" and enter the restored land. This is the activation of the prophesied New Covenant for Israel (Ezk. 36).

13. The Spirit of God will also someday pour out the blessing of the New Covenant on Gentiles as well as Jews (Joel 2).

14. When needed, the Holy Spirit can grant encouragement to those laboring under dire circumstances (Hagg. 2:5).

15. The Spirit was involved in the providence of restoration by protecting and being with the beleaguered Jews who had returned to Israel from Babylon (Zech. 4:6).

CHAPTER 4

THE HOLY SPIRIT IN THE GOSPELS

Introduction

The revelation concerning the Holy Spirit in the Old Testament is extremely sophisticated and complete. But, coming into the New Testament, there are many new major areas in which new information is revealed.

Just for example: (1) The Spirit's miraculous work in bringing about personal salvation. (2) The Spirit's permanent indwelling of believers, coupled with His ongoing work within the experience of that child of God. Walvoord carefully notes:

> *In the New Testament ... in contrast to the Old, a wider ministry of the Spirit is directed to the individual believer. Beginning at Pentecost the Spirit indwells every believer and constitutes a source of revelation concerning the will of God that before had been limited to a few. The Holy Spirit now guided, taught, and helped believers on a scale not found in the Old Testament. While revelation continued to follow its basic pattern, its effectiveness was greatly enlarged through this ministry of the Spirit.*[20]

In the New Testament there is an expansion and deeper revelation of what we have already noted: (1) More details about the deity of the Spirit of God, along with a fuller revelation of the doctrine of the Trinity. (2) The work of the Spirit in the life and ministry of Jesus as Messiah. (3) The work of the Spirit in the inspiration of the Word of God, through the apostles as instruments. (4) The work of the Spirit in the indwelling of believers on a permanent basis. (5) The giving of gifts to believers by the Spirit. (6) Specific positional work of the Spirit in the believer such as, the New Birth, Sanctification, Sealing work. (7) The convicting work of the Spirit whereby He convicts the world.

B. The Holy Spirit In The Gospels

The nation of Israel was under deep, dark spiritual oppression. The Romans ruled with an iron fist. The priests and Pharisees were choking the people with legalism. And the masses heard very little of the encouragement and blessings of the Lord. But God is about to do a new thing for Israel and for the world by sending His Son into the realm of mankind. Around 4 B.C., as many scholars calculate, Jesus would be born in Bethlehem!

Very early in the Gospels, the Holy Spirit began His ministry. (It must be remembered that the Gospels are recording for us the life of Christ, during the period of the Dispensation of the Law. The Dispensation of Grace would begin with the outpouring of the Spirit at Pentecost, Acts 2.) Pache points out:

> *The Gospels represent a period of transition in the Scriptures. Christ the Mediator of the New Covenant has come down to earth. By His words and His deeds He lays the basis of the future Dispensation which is only to begin after the crucifixion, the resurrection and the glorification of the Savior. The Church was not founded until Pentecost, by the descent of the Holy Spirit. In the Gospels, the result is that generally the teaching and promises of Jesus concerning the Spirit refer to the New Covenant, whereas the experiences realized by the forerunners and the disciples still belong to the Old. If we take careful note of this difference, we shall be guarded against confusion.*[21]

For the most part, the Gospels have to do with the revelation of and witness to Jesus as Messiah and Son of God. But too, the deity of Jesus and the Holy Spirit will also be brought to light in the Gospels of Matthew, Mark, Luke, and John. The Holy Spirit is vital in this important revelation witness to the nation of Israel!

C. The Spirit And John The Baptist

Isaiah 4.0:3 predicts one coming that would prepare the way of the Lord "in the wilderness." This desert prophet would be a "voice" who would call, *"Make smooth ... a highway for our God."* There would be a witness or forerunner who would dramatically herald the coming of the Messiah. He would come in the spirit and power of Elijah (Lu. 1:17). He would be called John the Baptizing one! And, the Holy Spirit would control him!

The book of Luke tells the story

Herod the Great is ruling over the Jewish people with a steel hammer. Under this oppressive background, God will send the Savior, His Son into the world. The Lord will reveal His gift of His Anointed One through some of the godliest men among the Jews.

Zecharias the priest and his wife Elizabeth were upwards in years. And, Elizabeth was a cousin to Mary who will give birth to Christ. Zecharias is visited by an angel who proclaims, *"Elizabeth will bear you a son, and you will give him the name John"* (Lu. 1:13). Further it was said: *"He will be great in the sight of the Lord, and he will drink no wine or liquor; and he will be filled (controlled) with the Holy Spirit, while yet in his mother's womb"* (1:15-16).

The Greek word for filled has the idea of control, as in contrast how, for example, wine would completely control a person's behavior. When he becomes mature, John will be moved and "controlled" by the Spirit of God. John will not be influenced by external motives or by any other human reasoning! God's Spirit will be this man's guide!

> *Not with wine but with the Holy Spirit will John be filled. This same implied contrast (filled with wine versus filled with the Holy Spirit) is found also in other passages (Acts 2:15-17, Eph. 5:18). John is not going to derive his strength or inspiration from earthly means but from the Holy Spirit.*[22]

Elizabeth, older and barren also, was controlled by the Holy Spirit (1:41) and Zecharias as well (v. 67). Zecharias had been struck with dumbness until the birth of his son. When the babe was born he had to write on a tablet the name "John." Those standing around were shocked and said, "but no one in your family has that name?" Yet, it was the Lord who wanted the child to have this name, which means "God is gracious." Immediately, the Spirit "controlled" John and he began to foretell that his son would be a "prophet of the Most High" (Lu. 1:76).

D. The Spirit And Mary

Mary would be very special in the eyes of the Lord. *"The favored one! The Lord is with you"* (Lu. 1:28).

There are several technical descriptions that explain the unique and miraculous nativity of Christ. And even with the clearest biblical explanations, we still cannot fathom the awesome fact of the Virgin Birth!

1. The Greek text puts it this way: *"[Mary] was discovered in the stomach (gastri) having, from the Holy Spirit"* (Matt. 1:18).

2. *"For that which was conceived (to be born) in her, is from the Holy Spirit"* (Matt. 1:20).

"The Holy Spirit will come upon you, and the power of the Most High will cast a shadow over you; thus for that reason the holy offspring shall be called the Son of God" (Lu. 1:35).

Early Genesis had forecast the virgin birth in the story of the Fall of Adam. Because of disobedience, the two would be cast from the presence of the Lord and would be thus needing a "redemption" that would take them back to God. Elohim said to Satan (who was embodying the serpent): *"I will put enmity between you and the woman, and between your seed and her seed; He [the seed of the woman] shall crush you [Satan] on the head, but you shall crush him on the heel"* (Gen. 3:15). Normally, generation is spoken of as coming through the male. But this cryptic prophecy speaks of the "seed" coming through the woman who would someday defeat Satan. The Messiah Jesus, virgin born, is clearly in view!

The virgin birth is specifically written about in Isaiah 7:14. The Hebrew word for virgin in this passage is *(almah)*, which is a specific technical term meaning: a young girl (in her teens) who is definitely a virgin and is of marriageable age. This perfectly fits Mary in the Gospel story.

E. The Spirit And The Presentation Of Jesus

Following the birth of Jesus, the Holy Spirit came upon a righteous man living in Jerusalem by the name of Simeon. He had been longing for the promised blessings to fall upon Israel as prophesied. Through the Spirit, he was promised *"he would not see death before he had seen the Lord's Messiah."* (Lu. 2:26).

Meanwhile, Mary and Joseph brought Jesus to the Temple so that a sacrifice of turtledoves could be made for Him, following the command of the Law of Moses.

At the same time, God's Spirit led Simeon to the Temple where he was given a glimpse of Christ with His parents. By the Holy Spirit, Simeon was led to cry out:

> *"My eyes have seen Your salvation, which You have prepared in the presence of all peoples, a light of revelation to the Gentiles, and the glory of Your people Israel"* (Lu. 2:29-32).

F. The Spirit Coming On Christ

Christ began His public ministry by appearing at the renegade and illegal baptisms of His cousin John.

> *Then Jesus arrived from Galilee at the Jordan coming to John, to be baptized by him* (Matt. 3:13).

The nation of Israel was cold in icy spiritual deadness. And the Lord used John to awaken the people to the desperate need for repentance and forgiveness. It would be John who would openly see the Holy Spirit alight on Christ!

> *And John bore witness saying, 'I have beheld the Spirit descending as a dove out of heaven, and He remained upon Him.' ... 'And I have seen, and have borne witness that this is the Son of God'* (Jo. 1:32, 34).

Since Jesus is indeed the second person of the Trinity, being very God, what is the significance of the Holy Spirit coming upon Him during His ministry here on earth? The Gospel accounts seem to give a variety of reasons. Much of it has to do with a witness to the people of Israel. The Holy Spirit would point to the fact that God's Son was here as promised in the Old Testament.

For example, John the Baptist says he bore witness that he saw *"the Spirit descending as a dove out of heaven, and He [the Spirit] remained [on*

Christ]" (Jo. 1:32). It was further revealed to John that, the One upon whom he sees the Spirit coming, this One would baptize (wash) the nation by means of this Holy Spirit, (1:33). John concludes, "*I have seen, and have borne witness that this is the Son of God*" (1:34). Whitelaw rightly points out:

> *The action and attitude of the dove were designed to symbolize the impartation to the baptized Christ of the fullness of the Spirit's influences that were requisite to fit His humanity to be the instrument or organ of His higher nature. ... The essential mark of Messiahship was not the external phenomenon, but the inward possession and outward manifestation by Christ of the fullness of the Spirit's power*[23]

Thomas farther says:

> *Christ was revealed to John by the Spirit, which descended from heaven like a dove. Up to that time, it would seem, he did not know [Christ]. At the baptism He was revealed to him in all the beauty of His character and the grandeur of His mission. Unless God reveals Christ to us, we cannot preach Him, How can we make Him known to others unless we know Him ourselves? And God must impart this knowledge; "flesh and blood" cannot reveal Him to us.*[24]

The Spirit was like an outward witness and confirmation that God was working with His Son. It must be remembered that the disciples (at least at first) only saw the humanity of Christ. The Holy Spirit coming upon the Son was a proof that He was carrying out the will of His Father, not simply His own "human" will. And yet later, we will see that Jesus the Son of God could also act upon His own power and by His own authority.

In discussions with some of his disciples, John the Baptist recognized the divine origins of Christ's deeds. He said in reference to Jesus, "*One can receive nothing, unless it has been given him from above*" (3:27). In other words, "*What Christ is doing comes from above.*" He then adds, "*He must increase, but I must decrease*" (3:30). He concludes, "*Whom God has sent speaks the words of God; for [the Lord] gives [His] Spirit without measure*" (3:34). That is, "*He has poured forth without restriction His Holy Spirit upon His Son!*"

John summarizes the power of the Spirit working in Jesus by saying, "*The Father loves the Son, and has given all things into His hand*" (3:35).

G. The Spirit And The Anointing Of Christ

Much later in New Testament history, as recorded in Acts, when Peter spoke with Cornelius and his household (Acts 10:34 - 48), he related how the Lord Jesus was *"anointed by the Holy Spirit"* (v. 38). Thus, Jesus' anointing meant He began operating by the power of the Spirit, with the result that He was *"doing good"* and *"healing all who were oppressed by the devil."* The Greek word anoint is (*xriw*) and is related to the word for Christ, (*xristos*). In the Old Testament, to give someone a vial of precious olive oil was a way to bless or favor that person. Olive oil softened and protected the skin from the intense heat of the climate. The idea to anoint later became the sign of the one blessed and favored, especially the one designated as king. (Xristos) then is "the Anointed One."

The Holy Spirit therefore, is the sign that Jesus is Israel's promised King! The end of verse 38 is interesting. It says, *"For God was with Him."* But too, the Holy Spirit is "with Him." Both the Spirit and the Father are working within the Son!

H. The Prophesied Baptism Of The Holy Spirit

The Old Testament Promises. The Old Testament describes many ceremonial baptisms (washings). A woman was to bathe or wash in reference to her menstrual period (Lev. 15). Elisha instructed Naaman to wash just prior to his miracle healing (II Kings 5:10). If someone touches a dead body, he must wash to be clean again (Lev. 11:36). Many other washings were required to cleanse a person after defilement.

With the coming of the promised New Covenant, the Covenant of the Law would be replaced (Jer. 31:31-37, and many other passages). Therefore, a spiritual washing done by the Holy Spirit would take place that would cleanse the nation of Israel. This will be far more important than simply a water ceremonial washing!

> Then I will *"slosh"* clean water on you, ... I will cleanse you from all your filthiness and from all your idols (Ezek. 36:25).

How will this happen? Two verses down Ezekiel quotes the Lord as saying: *"I will put My Spirit within you and cause you to walk in My statutes"* (36:27). This giving of the Spirit would bring about the "washing" and give spiritual life to the Jews. This prophecy was meant first for Israel. But this "New Covenant" promise would spill over to the Gentiles because God had prophesied even to Abraham that *"through you, all nations will be blessed"* (Gen. 12:3).

On Ezekiel 36 and 37, Walvoord writes:

> *In her restoration God would cleanse [Israel] and give her His Holy Spirit, ... The Holy Spirit will indwell them in that day in contrast to the Mosaic dispensation when only a few were indwelt. ... God would put His Holy Spirit in her and she would be settled in her own land.*[25]

> *"And I will put My Spirit within you, and you will come to life, and I will place you on your own land. Then you will know that I, the Lord, have spoken and done it, declares the Lord"* (37:14).

This "coming to life" is the new birth. The Jewish people would some-day be "born again" by the work of the Holy Spirit!

The prophet Joel foretold the pouring out of God's Spirit upon the Jews and upon all mankind (2:28-29). He writes: *"It will come about after this that I will pour out My Spirit on all mankind: ... I will pour out My Spirit in those days."*

This will be the Baptism of the Holy Spirit and the launching of the New Covenant at Pentecost, Acts 2!

I. Christ And The Baptism Of The Holy Spirit

John the Baptist told the Jews that his "washing" was but with the out-ward application of water (Matt. 3:11a). But he predicted that Jesus would *"baptize you with the Holy Spirit and fire"* (Matt. 3:11b).

By fire he meant judgment upon the nation. He explains this when he said *"And the axe is already positioned against the trees; every tree therefore that does not bear good fruit is cut down ..."* (3:10).

Thus, Jesus will do both. He will bring about the baptism of the Holy Spirit and, He will bring judgment upon Israel.

Two views on the judgment: 1) Some say this is future when Christ returns as King and judges the Jews. 2) Most feel it would come about when Israel almost totally rejected Jesus and His presentation of Himself to the nation. This makes the most sense because John made the issue of the "fire" as very near. *"The axe is already positioned against the tree."* At A.D. 70, the rejection of the nation was complete and judgment, with scattering, followed.

As we shall see later, this washing of the Holy Spirit will take place when the believing Jew under the New Covenant is placed into the spiritual Body of Christ. By becoming one with Him the Jews were to be washed and cleansed by being joined to the Lord's righteousness! This was predicted in concentrated form for Israel in Jeremiah and Ezekiel for the Jews in the Old Testament and repeated as a coming prophetic reality in the Gospels. It was clearly hinted at in Joel 2:28:

I will pour out My Spirit on all mankind; ...

Peter repeats this in Acts 2:17.

And as well, this truth was brought to pass and was fulfilled in Acts, concerning both Jew and Gentile! Then, it was explained theologically and doctrinally in the Epistles!

But More On This Baptism Of The Spirit In Paul's Writings Later!

J. The Spirit And The Temptation Of Christ

The story of Jesus being tempted by Satan in the wilderness has a distinct purpose. The purpose is to show that Christ the Son of God, living in our midst as human, could not fall under the power of sin and Satan, as sinful human beings can and do!

Some argue that the temptation may have not been real. It was simply a spiritual exercise but with little temptational teeth! But indeed the test was real!

God had a very providential purpose for this encounter. The dialogue tells us that Jesus was not an ordinary human being. He was the Son of God, obedient to His Father's will and under the immediate authority of the Spirit of God.

The Scriptures tell us Christ was "led up" by the Spirit in order to be tempted by Diabolos, or the Slanderer! (Matt. 4:1). Too, it adds that as He was taken into the desert, He was being "controlled" or filled (full, plaras) by the power of the Holy Spirit (Lu. 4:1).

Could not Christ by His own divine abilities resist Satan? Yes, but the point of the encounter is to show that Jesus was in total obedience to the Father, under the guidance of the Spirit! Through this event we know Christ was under the absolute will of the Father, as He was being controlled (filled) by the Spirit of God.

The question is often asked, could Jesus the Son of God, and deity Himself, withstand the temptations put upon Him? The question is answered by an old illustration: Can a rowboat actually attack a battleship? The answer is Yes! But the rowboat could not win. Jesus could be tempted but He could not sin because of His sinless nature as very God! In theology, this is called the doctrine of the *impeccability* of Christ.

The great Greek scholar John Albert Broadus (1827-1895) believes it was solely by the Spirit's power that Jesus was unable to sin. But this would possibly discount then the truth of the deity of Christ Himself and His own righteousness, and that He could just as well resist evil. The fact that Jesus could not sin is well supported by almost all Evangelical scholars. The Holy Spirit is with our Lord as a witness, and as an empowerment. But Christ was sinless in His own being. But Broadus' argument goes something like this:

> *How could Jesus be tempted? Was it possible for him to sin? If this was in no sense possible, then he was not really tempted, certainly not 'like as we are' (Heb. 4:15). But how can it have been possible for him to sin? If we think of his human nature in itself apart from the co-linked divinity, and apart from the Holy Spirit that filled and led him, then we must say that, like Adam in his state of purity ... [Jesus'] humanity was certainly in itself capable of sinning, and thus the temptation was real, and was felt as such, and as such overcome; while yet in virtue of the union with the divine nature, and of the power of the Holy Spirit that filled him, it was morally impossible that he should sin.[26]*

Walvoord rightly states:

> *The fact of the immutability of Christ is the first determining factor of His impeccability. According to Hebrews 13:8, Christ is 'the same yesterday and to-day, yea and for ever,' and earlier in the same epistle Psalm 102:2 7 is quoted, 'Thou art the same, and thy years shall not fail' (Heb. 1:12). As Christ was holy in eternity past, it is essential that this attribute as well as all others be preserved unchanged eternally. Christ must be impeccable, therefore, because He is immutable. If it is unthinkable that God could sin in eternity past, it must also be true that it is impossible for God to sin in the person of Christ incarnate. The nature of His person forbids susceptibility to sin.[27]*

In the historical account, Jesus goes 40 days without food. In the confrontation with the devil, the Lord uses Scripture to counter the propositions used against Him. During this period He is tried by Satan in three areas:

1. Trust-dependence. "*If You are the Son of God, command that these stones become bread*" (Matt. 4:3). Using Deuteronomy 8:3, Jesus answers, "*Man shall not live on bread alone, but on every word that proceeds out of the mouth of God*" (4:4).

2. Foolishly tempting God. *"If You are the Son of God throw Yourself down"* (Matt. 4:6). This time, Satan uses the Word of God and adds: *"He will give His angels charge concerning You"* (Ps. 91:11-12). The Lord answers with Deuteronomy 6:16: *"You shall not put the Lord your God to the test."*

3. Loyalty to God the Father. In the final encounter, Satan goes straight to the heart of the matter and says: *"All [the kingdoms of the world] will I give You, if You fall down and worship me"* (4:9). But Jesus again uses Scripture quoting Deuteronomy 6:13: *"You shall worship the Lord Your God, and serve Him only."*

With this, Satan retreats and angels came and began to minister to Christ (4:11). Toussaint concludes this account in his excellent commentary on Matthew:

> *The significance of the temptation is pointed out well by the Greek text. First of all, the phrase "was led up by the Spirit" indicates divine providence. It was not by reason of mere circumstances that Jesus was in the wilderness and was confronted with temptations by Satan. The passive verb with (upo) indicates Jesus was led by the Spirit into the wilderness. The passive infinitive "to be tempted" indicates a divine purpose.*[28]

K. The Spirit And The Disciples Of Christ

As Jesus ministered throughout the land of Israel, He assembled an inner core of twelve disciples and a larger company of about seventy. As the elders who worked with Moses, so these men would be given the Holy Spirit for special purposes. And those special purposes would be limited. However, it must be recognized that their overall spiritual maturity was limited as well. They did not witness as effectively as they could. Nor did they consistently draw upon the power of the Spirit. They certainly did not have Him residing within on an ongoing basis, as He would be later.

In Matthew 10, Christ gave the twelve authority over unclean spirits and disease (v. 1). He instructed them to go out and proclaim, *"The kingdom of heaven is at hand"* because the King has arrived! Most Bible teachers doubt if the disciples ever did draw upon or call to the Spirit of God.

But the Lord warned them of future persecution and rejection, and said when they begin to speak: *"it is not you who speak, but it is the Spirit of your*

Father who speaks in you" (10:20). Later He added:

> *When they arrest you and deliver you up, do not be anxious before-*
> *hand about what you are to say, but say whatever is given you in that*
> *hour; for it is not you who speak, but it is the Holy Spirit* (Mk. 13:11).

But looking to the time when He would be gone, Jesus promised that if they would ask the Father for the Holy Spirit, He would not withhold Him from coming within (Lu. 11:13).

After His resurrection, and anticipating the soon coming Dispensation of the Church, Jesus said to the twelve:

> *"Peace be with you; as the Father has sent Me, I also send you." And*
> *when He had said this, He breathed on them, and said to them,*
> *"Receive the Holy Spirit"* (John 20:21-22).

Some think that right then the disciples were given the Spirit. But better evidence suggests that Christ was referring to the giving of the Holy Spirit at Pentecost. The permanent indwelling was still future. Thus, His statement was near- prophetic! It was about to happen!

L. The Blaspheming Against The Spirit

Matthew 12:14-37 gives us the account of the blaspheming against the Holy Spirit. Many feel this can happen today. But it must be remembered that this encounter with the Pharisees, happened under the Dispensation of the Law when Christ was presenting Himself as King to the nation of Israel. It was prophesied to the Jews that the Messiah would heal; that He would perform objective, historical miracles among them. This would be the sign of His genuineness and that He has God's stamp upon His work.

In the context of the passage, the Pharisees, who were more than likely "lost" and did not belong to the Lord, had plotted to destroy Him (v. 14). They were angry when they saw the crowd opening their eyes to the fact that *"this man is the Son of David,"* in other words the promised Messiah (v. 23)!

What is interesting is that the Pharisees never doubted the healings of Christ, but instead, ascribed them to *"Beelzebub the ruler of the demons"* (v. 24).

In a certain sense, the Jews could deny Jesus as Messiah but they could not reject the plain, objective, historical, frontal witness of the Spirit. What was tragic was that they claimed the healings were from Beelzebub, the *"Lord of the flies,"* Satan! This could never be forgiven! Christ said that *"any sin and blasphemy shall be forgiven men, but blasphemy against the Spirit [in terms of what they had just seen], shall not be forgiven"* (v. 31).

Jesus reiterated the point again: *"Whoever shall speak a word against the Son of Man, it shall be forgiven him; but whoever shall speak against the Holy Spirit, it shall not be forgiven him, either in this age, or in the age to come"* (v. 32).

In reference to the nation of Israel's rejection of Christ, the writer of Hebrews notes, if they *"have fallen away, it is impossible to renew them again to repentance, since they again crucify to themselves the Son of Cod, and put Him to open shame"* (6:6). In the verses before, the author wrote of the "enlightenment" of Israel, how they had *"tasted of the heavenly gift and have been made partakers of the Holy Spirit"* (vs. 1-4). These words do not describe the personal salvation experience of an individual but the fact that Israel, as a nation, was granted the witness and the evidence that the Messiah was in their midst!

The Jewish rejection of that witness meant the ultimate scattering of the nation when Jerusalem was destroyed in A.D. 70.

M. The Spirit, Discipling And Witnessing

Then Jesus came to them and said, "All authority in Heaven and on Earth has been given to Me. Therefore go and make disciples of all nations, baptizing them in the name of the Father, and of the Son, and of the Holy Spirit" (Matthew 28:18-20).

Matthew 28:18-20 is often cited as the great Witnessing Command. Ironically, though witnessing must be part of the formula, the command really has in mind "discipling." The apostles were to make disciples "of all nations, baptizing them in the name of the Father and the Son and the Holy Spirit" (v. 19).

The grammatical construction of verse 19 gives us another key formula in the Doctrine of the Trinity. The word "name" is singular but the passage then describes "three persons," Father, Son and Spirit! With each noun, there is also the definite article "the." "The Father, The Son, The Spirit!"

Toussaint notes:

> *Not only does the Messiah claim to possess all authority, but He also places Himself on an equal level with the Father and the Holy Spirit. He instructs His disciples to baptize into the name of the Father, of the*

Son, and of the Holy Spirit. Finally, the King claims to be universally present with His own every day of the age (Matthew 28:20). [29]

N. The Spirit And The New Birth

The new birth is the central doctrine of the New Covenant. It is the core and heart of the salvation process. But there is also an aftermath to being "born again." The unfolding of the Christian's experience follows and the Spirit of God is the key to the entire process.

The book of John gives us more from the vantage point of the Gospels, about the new birth, than any of the other synoptic writings. Chapters 3, 6, 7, 14, 15, and 16 are definitive in understanding the salvation work and the part the Holy Spirit plays.

But a full picture of the Spirit's role in the New Birth process and, in the work of Soteriology in general, will be explained in more detail in the section on the Holy Spirit and the epistles.

CHAPTER 5

THE HOLY SPIRIT IN
THE BOOK OF ACTS

A. Introductions

The periods of the Dispensation of Law and of the Mosaic Covenant ended with the death of Christ. God made an open show of this, at the moment of Christ's death, when the great curtain in the Temple was torn from top to bottom.

> ... *darkness fell over the whole land until the ninth hour, the sun being obscured; and the veil of the temple was torn in two* (Lu. 23:44-45).

With the coming of the periods of the Dispensation of Grace, and of the New Covenant, the work of the Holy Spirit would take on new dimensions. But before going further the questions might be asked, "What is the Dispensation of Grace and the New Covenant?"

1. The New Covenant. This is a sub-covenant that expands and explains the blessing aspect of the Abrahamic Covenant given in Genesis

12. The Lord told Abraham, *"through you I will bless all families of the earth"* (v. 3). Jesus made it clear that with His impending death He would sign, seal and deliver the benefits of the New Covenant with His blood sacrifice.

> *After blessing [the Passover meal, Jesus broke the bread] and gave it to the disciples, and said, "Take, eat; this is My body." And when He had taken a cup and given thanks, He gave it to them, saying, "Drink from it, all of you; for this is My blood of the [new] covenant, which is poured out for many for forgiveness of sins"* (Matt. 26:26-28).

The New Covenant is a sovereign agreement and work of God whereby He provides salvation to mankind, because of the benefits offered through the death of His Son. The New Covenant is an extension of the Abrahamic Covenant from Genesis 12:3: *"Through you [Abram] I will bless all families of the earth."* Though it would first be given to the "natural" children of Abraham, because of the Genesis 12:3 promise, the New Covenant would spill over to bless the Gentiles. This is now taking place in this Dispensation of Grace.

On the New Covenant, and the fact that both Jew and Gentile benefit from it, Pentecost quoting Scofield and Lincoln writes:

> *'The New Covenant ... secures the perpetuity, future conversion, and blessing of Israel ... and it ... secures the eternal blessedness ... of all who believe.' ... Lincoln says: The blood of the New Covenant shed upon the cross of Calvary is the basis of all the blessings of the believer in the present age. The believer, therefore, participates in the worth to the sinner of the New Covenant, so that he partakes of the Lord's supper in remembrance of the blood of the New Covenant* (1 Cor 11:25), *and he is also a minister of the New Covenant* (II Cor. 3:6). *It is also said of the believer that he is a child of Abraham because he is of faith* (Gal. 3:7), *and of Christ* (Gal. 3:29). *He is also said to partake of the root and fatness of the olive tree* (Rom. 11:17). *So too, though as an unbelieving Gentile he is an 'alien' and a 'stranger'* (Eph. 2:19), *he is no longer such* (Eph. 2:29), *because he has been made nigh by the blood of Christ* (Eph. 2:13), *He benefits in the New Covenant as a fellow-citizen of the saints and of the household of God* (Eph. 2:19), *and not as a member of the commonwealth of Israel* (Eph. 2.12).
>
> *Grant says: ... we must remember that God is speaking here explicitly of His earthly people, and not of any heavenly one ... the people with whom this covenant will be made will be a people in that day*

entirely according to His mind. It will be asked how, according to this, the new covenant applies at all to us. Other scriptures answer this clearly by assuring us that if we have not the covenant made with us, it can yet, in all the blessings of which it speaks, be ministered to us.[30]

But the main elements of the New Covenant are given in Jeremiah and Ezekiel and, are meant for the nation of Israel first. In these passages we see the New Covenant interfacing with the Palestinian Covenant (the Jews' restoration to the Land), the Davidic Covenant (the Messiah reigning on His throne in Jerusalem). In Jeremiah 32:37-41 we see the three sub-covenants working together. They will bring about:

1.   A regathering of the Jews from all countries.

2.   A new personal relationship with the Lord.

3.   A new heart.

4.   The New Covenant is called an "everlasting" Covenant.

In Jeremiah 33, we see:

5.   God will keep His promise of blessing for Israel.

6.   The Messiah, the Branch, will execute righteousness in the land of Israel!

7.   The ordinances of nature guarantee the perpetuation of the Jewish people.

In Ezekiel 36-37, we see:

8.   Israel to be regathered from the nations.

9.   God will "slosh, splash, pour as from a bowl" clean water on Israel - a picture of spiritual washing. Later, related to the picture of baptism!

10. God will place His Spirit within the Jews.

11. As if resurrected from graves, Israel will again respond spiritually to God.

All three covenants will come together for Israel in the future millennium. However, the New Covenant (involving personal spiritual blessings) has already been ratified by Christ and launched by the Spirit at Pentecost.

And right now, at this moment, the New Covenant is the pavement, the road upon which the Lord works with humanity today. On top of the New Covenant God has inaugurated the Dispensation of Grace.

2. Dispensation Of Grace. For the last 2,000 years God has dealt with man in history by this Age or Economy of Graciousness! He waits patiently for men to turn to His Son for salvation. He withholds horrendous punitive judgment, giving humanity an opportunity for eternal redemption.

Both the New Covenant and the Dispensation of Grace started in the book of Acts by the outpouring of God's Holy Spirit.

3. The Transition Book. All scholars realize the book of Acts is recording for us a transition period, going from the Dispensation of the Law to the Dispensation of Grace. In this book, the Holy Spirit does some new and different things. Some of the works of the Spirit are confined only to this transition period. Other works will continue into the period of the Epistles and on into our day. But too, some will cease when the Church is fully established and moving forward in history.

Alexander notes:

> *The subject of the first part [of Acts] is the planting and the extension of the Church among the Jews by the ministry of Peter. The subject of the second [half] is the planting and extension of the Church among the Gentiles by the ministry of Paul.*[31]

B. Christ's Words Guided By The Spirit

The author of Acts, Dr. Luke the physician, records right at the first of the book that Christ's "orders" to His apostles were directed and guided by the Holy Spirit working in Him (Acts 1:2). Jesus does not need this guidance but it is a part of the Plan whereby He is obedient to the Father's will. Yet too, Jesus' will is supreme as well! Note the Spirit gave orders (1:2), and Jesus commanded (1:4).

[Jesus] after giving instructions through the Holy Spirit to the Apostles He had chosen (1: 2).

While [Jesus] was eating with them, He gave them this command: "Do not leave Jerusalem, but wait for the gift My Father promised, [the Holy Spirit], which you have heard Me speak about" (1:4).

Longenecker points out:

Apparently Luke also wanted to show through the word order of v. 2 that Jesus' mandate to witness was given to the apostles, who acted through the power of the Holy Spirit, whose coming was a direct result of our Lord's ascension. Each of these four factors - the witness mandate, the apostles, the Holy Spirit, the ascended Lord - is a major emphasis that runs throughout Acts; each receives special attention in chapters 1 and 2.[32]

C. The Baptism Of The Holy Spirit Predicted

Then, in chapter one of Acts, Christ repeats the early words of John the Baptist who prophesied that the Lord would *"baptize with the Holy Spirit"* (Matt. 3:11). This would be in contrast, of course, to John's baptism "with water" (Acts 1:5). It is interesting that Christ left off the phrase "and with fire" when He repeated the thoughts of John. The Lord is applying the Holy Spirit's baptism directly to the apostles. He leaves off the judgment issue concerning Israel. Indeed, that "fire" would soon fall on the nation of Israel and consume it from off the land (A.D. 70).

Later in I Corinthians 12, we will find that this Baptism of the Holy Spirit will actually place us into the spiritual body of Christ. This will actually by part and parcel of New Covenant salvation. Though the apostles were children of God by faith under the Dispensation of Law, they would transist into the spiritual body of Christ by the "cleansing work" of the Holy Spirit. This was prophesied in Ezekiel 36:25-27.

D. The Apostles Receiving "Ability" From The Holy Spirit

Along with this baptizing work of the Spirit, the disciples would also receive "power" (*dunamis*) or "ability" to witness from Jerusalem to the "remotest part of the earth" (1:8). And this would happen! Though James was martyred early, the rest of the disciples (except John) gave their lives in far flung countries and died for the truth of the Gospel. The Holy Spirit was working in them with this ultimate sacrifice of themselves! Simon J. Kistemaker correctly notes:

> *Only through the indwelling person and power of the Holy Spirit are the disciples able to witness for Jesus Christ. Not only the disciples receive the gift of the Spirit, but as Luke shows in Acts, numerous persons are filled with the Holy Spirit and become Christian witnesses. "Effective witness can be borne where the Spirit is, and where the Spirit is, effective witness will always follow." Jesus' word, "You will receive power" applies first to the twelve apostles and then to all believers who witness effectively for Jesus Christ.*[33]

E. The Spirit As Author Of Scripture

While the apostles were waiting for the Spirit to come, they returned to Jerusalem. As recorded in Acts, Peter felt it was important to replace one of their members, Judas, who had killed himself, following his betrayal of Christ. In the discussion that ensued, Peter speaks:

The Scripture had to be fulfilled, which the Holy Spirit foretold by the mouth of David concerning Judas (1:16).

Most believe Peter then alludes to Psalm 41:9:

> *Even my close friend, in whom I trusted, who ate my bread, has lifted up his heel against me.*

He also quotes Psalms 69:25 and 109:8:

> *Let his homestead be made desolate ... His office let another man take.*

What is important is the fact that the words of David and the Holy Spirit are considered the same. The Spirit is inspiring David and, it is as if when you read the words of one, you are reading the words of the other! Kistemaker adds:

> *[Peter] links the written Word to the Holy Spirit, who "spoke long ago through the mouth of David concerning Judas" (NIV). Scripture, then, is the product of the Spirit, as Peter eloquently states in one of his epistles (II Peter 1:20-21). He asserts that the Holy Spirit speaks by using the mouth of man. That is, the Spirit communicates to us through the mouth of David, the composer of many psalms.*[34]

G. The "Control" Of The Holy Spirit

The story of Acts 2 and Pentecost is familiar to all Christians. It is the fact of the pouring out of the Spirit and the beginning of the Church. But most do not know all that is really happening in this incredible passage. Much confusion abounds concerning Acts 2. Let's look at the sequence of events in order:

1. The Old Testament promised the coming indwelling of the Holy Spirit.

   I will put My Spirit within you, and you will come to life (Ezek. 37:14). *I will pour out My Spirit on all mankind* (Joel 2:28).

2. John the Baptist predicted that Jesus would someday baptize the people by the Holy Spirit (Matt. 3:11).

3. Christ refers to John and tells His disciples that the promised baptism of the Spirit was near. He adds "not many days from now" (Acts 1:5). Following our Lord's ascension, the apostles wait for the coming of the Holy Spirit as they were told. Then came Pentecost.

The festival of Pentecost received its name from its occurring on the fiftieth day from the second day of the Passover; so that the interval embraced a circle of seven entire weeks. Its observance took place at the close of the gathering of the harvest. This occasion was providential for the outpouring of God's Spirit upon those who trust Him. The Spirit would reap a harvest of souls for the name of Christ!

What actually happened in Acts 2:1-4 during this festival of Pentecost? Two things took place specifically, though one event is directly mentioned and the other is not. The passage actually reads:

When the day of Pentecost had come, they were all together in one place (most believe at the Temple site). And suddenly there came from heaven a noise like a violent, rushing wind, and it filled the whole house where they were sitting. And there appeared to them tongues as of fire distributing themselves, and they rested on each one of them. And they were all filled with the Holy Spirit and began to speak with other tongues, as the Spirit was giving them utterance.

Several important things to notice:

1. Noise, Fire. The passage says a noise was heard like a rushing wind. A wind did not actually blow. But a mighty noise was heard! Tongues (or languages) fell on them as of fire. This gift of languages spread rapidly from one to another as a wild, fast moving brush fire! The gift of language (*glossa*) was foreign speech and specific dialects (*dialektos*, v. 8). This gift was given to the disciples and others sovereignly in order that the gospel might be witnessed to among Jews and Gentile proselytes who had come to Jerusalem for pilgrimage from other lands. They would all hear the testimony of Jesus in their own homegrown dialects and would return and tell thousands in other places that the Messiah was crucified and now is risen from the grave! Kistemaker adds:

> The coming of the Spirit fulfills John the Baptist's prophecy that the disciples would be baptized with the Spirit... Therefore the coming of the Holy Spirit ushers in a new era, for he comes to take up his dwelling with men not temporarily but forever. ... The Greek text indicates that the filling with the Spirit occurred once for all. That is, the Spirit did not come and go but stayed, as is evident from Luke's account. ... The Christian who is filled with the Spirit becomes the Spirit's mouthpiece. In the case of the believers in Jerusalem, they speak in other tongues and thereby prove that the Holy Spirit controls and enables them. The word tongue is the equivalent of the concept-spoken language. This is evident from Luke's comment that "each one was hearing them speaking in his own language."[35]

When "filling" is mentioned throughout Acts, other things happen besides the activation of the gift of languages. We will see what takes place in later passages. But it is false to say "the filling of the Spirit with the evidence of speaking in tongues," as if that is what always happens. It does not!

2. Filling. That the disciples were "filled" (*plarow*) by the Holy Spirit is stated clearly. The mistaken view is that the Spirit fills the believer like you "fill up" a glass with water. The contextual idea is that the Spirit "controls" the believer and uses him for a special purpose.

3. Spirit Baptism. Unstated in chapter 2 of Acts is the fact that the apostles and other believers, who were part of this group, were *"baptized by the Holy Spirit."* This would be the official placing of these believers into the spiritual body of Christ. Peter looks back on Acts 2 in later chapters and calls what happened here the Spirit's baptism.

For example, when the Spirit fell on the Gentiles at Cornelius' house, Peter said they *"have received the Holy Spirit just as we did"* (10:47). Later at Jerusalem Peter repeats what happened with Cornelius and friends and adds:

> *And I remembered the word of the Lord how He used to say, "John baptized with water, but you shall be baptized with the Holy Spirit"* (11: 16).

He further says that as he began to speak in that home "the Holy Spirit fell upon them, *just as he did upon us at the beginning"* (11:15).

Peter identified all this working of the Spirit as the "baptism." But too, the "filling" or "controlling" of the Spirit happened at the same time, though the two are actually different! These are actually two distinct works of God's Holy Spirit in the lives of believers.

G. What Else Does Acts Say About The Spirit's "Controlling?"

In Acts, this controlling is a sovereign work of the Holy Spirit. It just happens as the Spirit works with different ones. In the Epistles the "filling" of the Spirit is only mentioned once, and that happens to be in the book of Ephesians. There, believers are commanded to be "daily" controlled by Him. *"Be continually controlled by the Spirit"* (Eph. 5:18). (Greek: "controlled," Present tense command.) We who are now living past the launch stage of the Church are responsible and aware of this ongoing work. It is not automatic as in the transitional book of Acts. Notice the variety of things that happen in Acts when the Spirit "controls" either the apostles or the average believer:

> *"Peter, controlled by the Holy Spirit, said to them"* (4:8). Notice Peter simply spoke. He did not speak with a language.

> *"And they were all controlled by the Holy Spirit, and began to speak the word of God with boldness"* (4:31).

> The first Church needing leadership was to seek out and find *"seven men of good reputations full of the Spirit and of wisdom"* (6:3).

> *"They chose Stephen, a man full of faith and of the Holy Spirit"* and others (6:5).

Just before Stephen was martyred, it was said that he was *"full of the Holy Spirit"* so that he might see Christ glorified at the right hand of God the Father in heaven (7:55).

Following Paul's traumatic conversion on the Damascus road, he was brought before a believer in Christ, Ananias. The text says that then Paul was *"controlled with the Holy Spirit"* (9:17). Immediately he began to proclaim the gospel in the synagogues saying Jesus *"is the Son of God"* (9:20).

It was said of Barnabas that *"he was a good man, and full of the Holy Spirit and of faith"* (11:24).

Saul (Paul) challenged Elymas, saying he was full of deceit and a son of the devil. As Paul spoke he fixed his gaze on this man for Paul *"was controlled"* with the Holy Spirit (13:9).

The disciples were continually *"controlled"* with joy and with the Holy Spirit (13:52).

H. The Holy Spirit And Joel 2

The two main passages describing the Holy Spirit coming as part of the New Covenant are: Ezekiel 36:25-27; 37:14; 39:29; Joel 2:28-32. The New Covenant is an extension of the Abrahamic Covenant, in particular Genesis 12:3: *"And through you [Abraham] all the families of the earth shall be blessed."*

This New Covenant will replace the Mosaic Covenant (the Law):

> *Behold, the days are coming, declares the Lord, when I will make a new covenant with the house of Israel and with the house of Judah, not like the covenant which I made with their fathers in the day I took them by the hand to bring them out of the land of Egypt, My covenant [the Law] which they broke, although I was a husband to them, declares the Lord* (Jer. 31:31-32).

This New Covenant foreshadowed a closer, personal relationship with the Lord, a permanent forgiveness of sins, and the permanent indwelling of the Spirit of God:

I will be their God, and they shall be My people (Jer. 31:33b).

I will forgive their iniquity, and their sin I will remember no more (31:34b).

I will pour out My Spirit on all mankind (Joel 2:28).

Notice the passage says "on all mankind." The Hebrew is "upon all flesh." When Peter quotes Joel 2:28-32a in Acts 2:16-21, he said in v. 17 in Greek (*pasan sarka*) or "each kind of humanity [flesh]." (The NAS translates it "My Spirit upon all mankind.")

Notice as well that Peter quotes the whole paragraph from Joel 2:28-32a. He includes the verses that speak of *"wonders in the sky above, and signs on the earth beneath, blood, and fire, and vapor of smoke. The sun shall be turned into darkness, and the moon into blood, before the great and glorious day of the Lord shall come."*

These events of terror and tribulation are yet future. But the pouring out of the Holy Spirit on "mankind" (Jew and Gentile) took place here in Acts. Peter makes this clear when he said: *"This is what was spoken of through the prophet Joel."*

The coming of the Holy Spirit launches the New Covenant. And as well, the Dispensation of Grace (or the Church Age) begins. It would shortly be made up of Jew and Gentile.

What Joel said would happen when the Spirit of God was poured forth did indeed take place in Acts:

Your sons and daughters shall prophesy. *"Now [Philip] had four virgin daughters who were prophetesses"* (21:9). *"Some prophets came down from Jerusalem to Antioch"* (11:27).

Your young men shall see visions; your old men shall dream dreams. *"The Lord said to [Ananias] in a vision"* (9:10). *"[Cornelius] clearly saw in a vision an angel of God"* (10:3). *"[Peter] fell into a trance; and he beheld the sky opened up"* (10:10-11).

Who Sends the Holy Spirit?

As Peter continues to speak in Acts 2, he says that it is the exalted Christ who sends the Spirit:

[Christ], having been exalted to the right hand of God, and having received from the Father the promise of the Holy Spirit, He [Jesus] has poured forth this [the Spirit] which you both see and hear (2:23).

The Son sends the Spirit, as promised from the Father. Jesus said that the Spirit will come, as sent by Himself and the Father:

The Helper, the Holy Spirit [will come], whom the Father will send in My name (John 14:26).

When the Helper comes, whom I will send to you from the Father, that is the Spirit of truth (John 15:26).

I. Was The Holy Spirit Held Back From Believers In Acts?

In 19:1-7, the apostle Paul ran into twelve "disciples" of John the Baptist. Paul asked, *"Did you receive the Holy Spirit when you believed?"* The men answered, *"We have not even heard whether there is a Holy Spirit."* Obviously, these are primitive believers who believed what they had heard concerning repentance in regard to the message of John. Paul found these disciples near Ephesus, a far distance from Palestine where John had ministered years before.

Were these men Jews who had been in Judea and had seen John or Jesus? Were they Greeks who just got the message late about the ministry of John all the way from Israel? Or, were they Jews living in Greece who received a late word about John's work in the desert?

I believe they had responded to John's call for repentance, even if they had never been in Palestine. But they were then "saved" in an Old Testament context. The New Testament belief context would be to put personal faith in Christ as Savior. According to what we have already seen in Acts these men, if they had earlier heard about Jesus and had put trust in Him, would have then "automatically" received the Spirit of God who would have come into their lives.

But that did not happen. They were in the dark, in regard to the Messiah's death, burial and resurrection for their sins. It took the apostles, such as Paul, to "confirm" that these disciples truly were saints, even in an Old Testament context.

Paul then confirms their belief:

When Paul had laid his hands upon them, the Holy Spirit came on them, and they began speaking with languages and prophesying (19:6).

Since they were near Ephesus and in the midst of a language melting pot, they began to speak with other "languages" as a witness.

Something similar had happened earlier in Samaria. More on this in coming pages.

Important

Today there is no delay in the Receiving of the Holy Spirit at the Point of belief!

Stanley Toussaint rightly summarizes:

Normally the Holy Spirit baptizes, indwells, and seals at the moment of faith, but in this instance the delay served several purposes: (1) Peter and John 's prayer (for bestowing of the Holy Spirit) and their laying on of hands (resulting in the coming of the Spirit) confirmed Philip's ministry among the Samaritans. This authenticated this new work to the Jerusalem apostles. (2) Also this confirmed Philip's ministry to the Samaritans. (3) Perhaps the most important aspect of God's withholding the Spirit till apostolic representatives came from the Jerusalem church was to prevent schism. Because of the natural propensity of division between Jews and Samaritans it was essential for Peter and John to welcome the Samaritan believers officially into the church.[36]

Because there is a transition under way in Acts going from the Dispensation of Law to the Dispensation of Grace, some for specific reasons received the Spirit after their salvation experience. This happens only a few times in the book. It was not the normative experience and is certainly not so now that the Church has been established.

1. The Disciples. The disciples were "saved" in Old Testament terminology but had to wait following Christ's ascension before receiving the Spirit (Acts 2). Jesus had told them, *"You shall be baptized with the Holy Spirit not many days from now"* (1:5).

2. The Samaritans. To the north and west of Jerusalem is the area called Samaria. The people living there were half Jewish and half Assyrian. The Assyrians had migrated to this area following 722 BC, after that nation had invaded the Northern Kingdom Israel. Thus, the people were half-breeds and despised by the "pure" Jews of other parts of the land. A religious Jew would not pass through Samaria.

Philip journeyed to Samaria and *"began proclaiming Christ to them"* (Acts 8:5). And:

> *When [the Samaritans] believed Philip preaching the good news about the kingdom of God and the name of Jesus Christ, they were being baptized [in water], men and women alike* (8:12).

The biblical text tells us in Acts 8: 14-17:

> *Now when the apostles in Jerusalem heard that Samaria had received the word of God, they sent them Peter and John, who came down and prayed for them, that they might receive the Holy Spirit. For He had not yet fallen upon any of them; they had simply been baptized in the name of the Lord Jesus. Then they began laying hands upon any of them; and they were receiving the Holy Spirit.*

Apparently, the apostles were concerned about the conversion of the Samaritans being real. Because the Samaritans were half-breeds and not fully Jews, they wanted to make sure they understood the "new" message, the prophecies and what it meant to accept Christ. The apostles had the authority to bestow the Holy Spirit.

But the actual practice of this even in Acts is rare. Several things to note:

1) These Samaritans indeed had trusted the Lord. They had no problem accepting what Paul was saying. They were ripe for the transition.

2) Apostolic authority again is very important in this passage. Paul confirmed that they had understood the message of Christ correctly. Thus, the Spirit came as Paul laid his hands upon them.

3) It would be a mistake to assume that the speaking with languages and prophesying is now normative for all accepting Christ. This is absolutely not true and in fact, as has already clearly been pointed out,

is even extremely rare in the book of Acts.

Some today want to say the laying on of hands, and the gifts of language and prophesying are the necessary signs of salvation. But they are those who are not looking thoroughly at all the Scriptures. Many today desire the signs of power! Too, they need the security of some kind of evidence. They are actually flying against what the rest of Acts shows us and what the epistles of Paul and Peter teach us!

J. The Holy Spirit Working Through The Twelve And Other Disciples

1. Philip. The Holy Spirit "directly" directed Philip in his evangelism mission, In Acts 8:26-40; he was told to go south from Jerusalem to Gaza. The Lord wanted him to witness to an Ethiopian official of the court of Candace, queen of Ethiopia.

Surprisingly, Philip is directed by an angel of the Lord who spoke clearly to him (v. 26). But too, the Spirit said to him, *"Go up and join this chariot [of the eunuch]"* (v. 29).

After Philip had led the man to a saving relationship with Christ, and after the man is baptized, *"The Spirit of the Lord snatched Philip away; and the eunuch saw him no more, but went on his way rejoicing"* (v. 39).

2. Peter. Before Peter went to Cornelius' home, the Spirit told him, *"Behold, three men are looking for you"* (10:19). These men would take Peter to Cornelius. Later, back in Jerusalem, Peter recounts this event to the disciples and says: *"The Spirit told me to go with them without misgivings"* (11:12).

3. Agabus. In the transition period of the book of Acts, God used many prophets as teachers to help establish the New Testament Church. Agabus was used of the Lord to warn the early church of a coming world famine. This evidently prepared the people as to where they should go when this disaster hit. Acts 11:28 tells us:

> *Agabus stood up and began to indicate by the Spirit that there would certainly be a great famine all over the world. And this took place in the reign of Claudius.*

Again, he is used by the Spirit of God in warning that the Jews of

Jerusalem would arrest Paul and turn him over to the Gentiles. Agabus took Paul's belt and tied it around his own hands and feet and declared: "This is what the Holy Spirit says: in this way the Jews at Jerusalem will bind the man who owns this belt" (21:11). Paul accepted these words as sealing his fate. He knew God directed his going to Jerusalem and that he would ultimately pay the supreme price!

4. Barnabus and Simeon. At Antioch, these two men, plus others, and including Paul (Saul), were praying, fasting and ministering to the Lord. Suddenly the Holy Spirit spoke and directed a new path for this small new group. The Spirit said, *"Set apart for Me Barnabas and Saul for the work to which I have called them"* (13:3). The Spirit then directed them to Seleucia (v. 4).

Note the personal pronoun "Me." The Spirit is indeed Person and can and did direct the early church leaders for His own designs. Of course those designs are in total conformity to the will of the Father as well!

5. "Other" Disciples. The Spirit spoke to and through other disciples besides the chief disciples! As Paul was on his way back to Jerusalem, he was warned by other disciples "through the Spirit not to set foot in Jerusalem" (Acts 21:4). Some feel Paul was hardheaded in going on to the city. But this warning is more of a reminder of what is going to happen, as first mentioned to him back in Acts 20:23: *"The Holy Spirit solemnly testifies to me in every city, saying that bonds and afflictions await men."* What Paul is saying is that everywhere he went the Spirit put on the hearts of others this fact of affliction awaiting him.

Paul's answer was: "I do not consider my life of any account as dear to myself" (20:24). In the course of time, these first steps back to Jerusalem would mean his arrest and his eventual martyrdom in Rome!

6. The Apostles and Elders. When the apostles and elders at Jerusalem commissioned Paul and Barnabas for teaching in Antioch, a letter was written from them to the church there. The letter made it clear that the Gentiles would not be under the Law in order to be accepted as true believers in Christ. Too, the letter speaks of the co-approval concerning this issue from the Jerusalem body, but apparently the Spirit confirmed it. The letter reads, *"For it seemed good to the Holy Spirit and to us to lay upon you no greater burden than these essentials: that you abstain from things sacrificed to idols and from blood and from things strangled and from fornication"* (15:28-29).

Ultimately, all church elders are led of the Holy Spirit to their position of overseer (*episcopos*: "to look over or beyond, to scope out carefully") (Acts 20:28). Paul told the Ephesian elders:

> *Be on guard for yourselves and for all the flock, among which the Holy Spirit has made you overseers, to shepherd the church of God which He purchased with His own blood.*

Note another Trinitarian formula: *"God purchased with His own blood!"* At first it would seem as if there is a Greek grammar or textual mistake. But it is not! Christ is God! It is God the Son who purchased our salvation!

Paul and Silas were openly and directly led of the Spirit not to travel for a time to Asia (Acts 16:6). In describing this incident, Paul tells us it was *"the Spirit of (or from) Jesus that did not permit them [to go]"* (16:7). Or, it may read, *"the Spirit related to Jesus."* This is another proof of the Trinitarian formula that is so consistent in the Scriptures!

Finally, as Paul recounts his testimony as to how God directed his ministry, he shares the way the Holy Spirit directed him in every city he visited. But the Spirit as well shared with Paul his coming fate of ultimate martyrdom. He says:

> *"The Holy Spirit solemnly testifies to me in every city, saying that bonds and afflictions await me. But I do not consider my life of any account as dear to myself, in order that I may finish my course, and the ministry which I received from the Lord Jesus, to testify solemnly of the gospel of the grace of God"* (Acts 20:23-24).

K. The Spirit "Counsels" The Churches

In John 14:16, 26; 15:26 Jesus says that He and the Father will send the (*paraklatos*, One called alongside), the Counselor, to indwell forever those who are His. By this indwelling, He would assist believers *"to bear witness"* (15:27).

Acts 9:31 tells us that *"the church throughout all Judea and Galilee and Samaria enjoyed peace, being built up' and, going on in the fear of the Lord and in the comfort (paraklasei, Counseling) of the Holy Spirit"* What Christ predicted, was happening in the churches in those areas. The Spirit of God was greatly moving with the believers because the verse further says the church *"continued to increase."* The Spirit was granting comfort to the churches and giving them purpose.

CHAPTER 6

THE HOLY SPIRIT AND THE DOCTRINE OF SALVATION

A. Introduction

The New Covenant as well as the Dispensation of Grace both began in the book of Acts. But we have reserved mentioning details of how the Holy Spirit works in Salvation. The reason: this should be treated in its entirety. The whole compass of salvation needs to be studied as a whole. Though the Baptism (Washing) of the Spirit has been touched on, it needs to be studied in the full light of the epistles. But there are some extremely important verses in the book of John we can begin with. They lead us into the full doctrine of the Spirit's work in the writings of Paul and Peter.

In the salvation process the Spirit:

1. Creates new life
2. Baptizes the believer into the spiritual body of Christ
3. Seals the child of God for eternity

The dynamic for the coming earthly Messianic Kingdom is the New Covenant. Though first prophesied for Israel, its benefits will bring salvation to the Gentiles. The New Covenant includes: 1) permanent forgiveness of sins, 2) a new heart, 3) the Law written on the heart, 4) a cleansing (washing), 5) the Holy Spirit giving new life [being born again], 6) the Holy Spirit dwelling within.

B. Creates New Life

Through Ezekiel, God promised to the Jews a new heart and a new Spirit (36:26). Then He adds: *"I will put My Spirit within you"* (v. 27). In the process the Lord adds: *"I will cause breath to enter you that you may come alive"* (37:5). And, *"I will put My Spirit within you, and you will come to life"* (v. 14).

For the Jews, this new life is for their ultimately living in the coming earthly Kingdom. *"I will place you on your own land"* (v. 14).

Jesus introduced the New Covenant and the Kingdom when He was here on earth. The Jewish people as a whole rejected the King and His reign. But when our Lord made His sacrifice for sins, He signed, sealed, delivered and initiated the New Covenant for Israel and for Gentiles. Just before His arrest, trials, and crucifixion, He told His disciples as they were celebrating Passover, *"This cup [of wine] which is poured out for you is the new covenant in My blood"* (Luke 22:20).

The New Covenant was then launched or given at Pentecost, Acts 2.

During this Dispensation of the Church Age, the Gentiles will be the main recipients of the New Covenant. The Jews are now judicially blinded, though some are continually brought to Christ. But God soon will restore the Jews to their promises and to their land. The Holy Spirit will move on them and they will accept their Messiah. This will be the work of the Spirit applying the New Covenant to Israel.

The land promises are not given to future Gentile believers, but some distant generation of Jews will be "born again" and indeed be led into the historic Davidic Kingdom!

(Though saved people from all Gentile nations will be there, in the Kingdom, and they will see a remnant of the Jewish people who had accepted Jesus as their King and Savior. Too, Old Testament Jewish saints will be resurrected and will be there to enjoy their promised Messiah!)

Christ mentions this issue of being born again in John 3.

In John 3 Nicodemus, apparently a member of the Sanhedrin and ruling body of Israel comes to Christ to ask what must have been ongoing questions by the people in regard to the prophesied literal Davidic reign and rule. We believe this because Jesus gives a direct answer about the Kingdom, *"Truly, truly, I say to you, unless one is born again, he cannot see the kingdom of God."* (3:3).

Nicodemus' point of reference would only have been this literal, earthly Davidic reign of the Messiah!

But what is this born again stuff! Nicodemus does not understand and says: *"How can a man be born when he is old? He cannot enter a second time into his mother's womb and be born, can he?"* (v. 4). Jesus gives the key answer:

> *Unless one is born of water and the Spirit, he cannot enter into the kingdom of God* (v. 5).

Since the passage has one preposition (of) controlling two nouns (water, Spirit) that are joined by a conjunction (and), the better reading is:

> *Unless one is born of water even, or that is the Spirit.*

Almost all scholars believe Christ is referring to Ezekiel 36:25-27.

> *Then I will slosh, pour clean water on you, I will cleanse you from all your filthiness and from all your idols. I will put My Spirit within you.*

Can water really cleanse from spiritual filthiness? The answer is a loud no! And the Jews well knew this fact. Thus, the water is not literal but, by the statements of Christ in John 3, that water would refer to the work of the Spirit!

Jesus further adds in that passage that it is one thing to be born, humanly speaking, by flesh. It is another thing to be spiritually born of the Holy Spirit (v. 6). As well, the Spirit is sovereign. He goes where He will. *"The wind blows where it wishes ... so is everyone who is born of the Spirit."* (v. 8).

Remember, this being "born again" was predicted in Ezekiel 37. *"I will put My Spirit within you, and you will come to life"* (v. 14).

Christ again mentions the inner work of the Spirit in John 7. On the last day of the Feast of Booths, Jesus cried out:

"If any man is thirsty, let him come to Me and drink. He who believes

in Me, as the Scripture said, 'From his innermost being shall flow rivers of live water.' But this He spoke of the Spirit, whom those who believe in Him were to receive; for the Spirit was not yet given, because Jesus was not yet glorified" (vs. 37-39).

When Christ stated, "as the Scripture said" He was probably referring to Isaiah 44:3-4 that reads:

I will pour out My Spirit on your offspring, and My blessing on your descendants, and they will spring up among the grass ... One will say, 'I am the Lord's

After Jesus had explained being born again, Nicodemus asks, *"How can these things be?"* (3:9).

Jesus answered and said to him, 'Are you the teacher of Israel, and do not understand these things?'

The only place in the Old Testament He could be referring to would be Ezekiel 36-37!

The Lord again refers to the work of the Spirit in giving life in John 6:63:

It is the Spirit who gives life; the flesh profits nothing; the words that I have spoken to you are spirit and are life.

Paul picks up on the issue of the new birth and writes in Titus 3:5:

[God] saved us, not on the basis of deeds which we have done in right- eousness, but according to His mercy, by the washing or regeneration and renewing by the Holy Spirit.

The text better reads: *"by the washing of the again - birth even the remaking of the Holy Spirit."*

Ezekiel saw Israel as dead bodies and dry bones (ch. 37). Paul likewise says, *"you were dead in your trespasses and sins"* (Eph. 2:1). He adds, but God *"made us alive together with Christ"* (2:5).

(Note God the Father makes alive and the Holy Spirit makes alive!)

C. The Sealing Of The Holy Spirit

Once one is born again, the Holy Spirit becomes a seal and a pledge concerning our ultimate and future redemption. Paul writes:

"Having also believed, you were sealed [in Christ] with the Holy Spirit of promise" (Eph. 1:13).

As well, Paul says the Spirit *"is given as a pledge of our inheritance, with a view to the redemption of God's own possession, to the praise of His glory"* (1:14).

In biblical days a seal verified an official decision. It was a form of a guarantee in regard to the command of the king or an administrator of the realm. Seals were the "signatures" that proclaimed a royal order, in reference to various official issues. For example, when Daniel was cast to the lions, king Darius was required by his own law to carry out the sentence of death against the man he so admired. The text tells us:

"The king sealed [the mouth of the lions' den] with his own signet ring and with the signet rings of his nobles, so that nothing might be changed in regard to Daniel" (Dan. 6:17).

Because the Holy Spirit is our Seal, nothing can be changed in regard to our salvation until we are finally redeemed (released) to go home to glory! (Eph. 1:14).

The Spirit of God is also our Pledge. The word means *"first installment, down payment, guarantee."* The Holy Spirit is our surety, the promised arrangement that "assures" our destiny in heaven.

With the Spirit as our seal and pledge, we are eternally secure in our position with God. This is why Paul writes that in the Lord's eternal viewpoint, already in heaven!

We have been given every spiritual blessing because we are in the *"heavenly places with Christ"* (Eph. 1:3). And Paul repeats: *"[God] raised us up with [Christ], in the heavenly places, with Christ Jesus"* (2:6).

D. Baptism (Washing) Of The Holy Spirit

In the Old Testament, ritual washing was seen as an outward sign of an inner cleansing. Of course the Old Testament was pointing forward when God would truly cleanse within by His Spirit. We've already noted references that refer to the coming Washing of the Holy Spirit as a signification of the work of the New Covenant within the individual believer. In Acts we read:

> [Christ speaking]: "You shall be baptized with the Holy Spirit not many days from now" (1:5).

> [Peter speaking]: "I remembered the word of the Lord, how He used to say, 'John baptized with water, but you shall be baptized with the Holy Spirit'" (11:16).

In Paul's epistles he makes at least three direct references to this spiritual baptism whereby he says we are united with the spiritual body of Christ. The apostle Peter makes at least one clear reference in his writings.

Paul:

> 1. For even as the body is one and yet has many members, and all the members of the body, though they are many, are one body, so also is Christ. For by one Spirit we were all baptized into one body, whether Jews or Greeks, whether slaves or free, and we were all made to drink of one Spirit (I Cor 12:12-13).

Paul emphasizes the unity that is the result of this baptism. Some think this refers to water baptism and that it unites believers to a local church. But this is not so. This is the work of God's Spirit at the point of belief. We are never commanded to be baptized by the Spirit. Paul even says later this work of the Holy Spirit is what unites us to Christ whereby we receive salvation.

Note too, from this I Corinthians passage, we all become equal in Christ. There needs to be a note of caution on this point, however. There is still rank and order in the church and in the family. In a democratic army, the general and the private are equal as citizens but they are not equal in terms of the structure of the military.

(In another chapter, we will deal with the result of the Baptism of the Spirit and that is, the giving of the spiritual gifts.)

> 2. Do you not know that all of us who have been baptized into Christ Jesus have been baptized into His death? Therefore we have been buried with Him through baptism into death, in order that as Christ was raised from

the dead through the glory of the Father, so we too might walk in newness of life. For if we have become united with Him in the likeness of His death, certainly we shall be also in the likeness of His resurrection (Rom. 6:3-4).

Some wrongly think the baptism in this passage is a reference to literal water baptism. Then it would follow that we are literally buried together with Christ? No. What Paul is saying is that God "sees" us so related to Jesus, that we spiritually go with Him through the process of death, burial and resurrection. Some of us may even escape death, if taken home by the Rapture. However, other passages certainly tell us that we shall indeed experience a literal resurrection, just as Christ was literally and historically brought forth from the grave.

John Winner notes:

> *The question here is whether Paul had in mind Spirit baptism* (I Cor. 12:13) *or water baptism. Some object to taking Romans 6:3 as Spirit baptism because that verse speaks of being "baptized into Christ" whereas I Corinthians 12:13 speaks of Spirit baptism placing the believer into Christ's body. Of course, both are true: the believer is "baptized" (placed into) Christ and also into the body of Christ, and both are done by the Holy Spirit.*[37]

> 3. *In Him you were also circumcised with a circumcision made without hands, in the removal of the body of flesh by the circumcision of Christ; having been buried with Him in baptism, in which you were also raised up with Him through faith in the working of God, who raised Him from the dead* (Col. 2:11-12).

Is this a literal circumcision? No. Neither is the baptism mentioned in this passage. Neither have I yet been raised with Christ literally, though Paul says I have been raised with Him in God's timeless view of all things! What does the apostle mean by all of this? Just this, that God saw me spiritually united with Christ in this spiritual baptism. We know from I Corinthians 12 that it is the dynamic work of the Holy Spirit!

Peter:

> 4. *For Christ also died for sins once for all, the just for the unjust, in order*

that He might bring us to God, having been put to death in the flesh, but made alive by the Spirit (I Pet. 3:18).

Peter goes on and describes how Christ, between His death and resurrection, went to the place of the dead and proclaimed to the Noahic generation the Gospel or the patience of God, with that generation, before the flood waters covered the earth (vs. 19-20a). Peter then says Noah and his family were brought *"safely through the water"* (v. 20b).

Peter then calls the event of Noah and his family being saved as through water, a type (Tupo). He says:

And relating to that, a type, [whereby] baptism now saves you - not the removal of dirt from the flesh, but an appeal to God for a good conscience - through the resurrection of Jesus Christ (v. 21).

Though a difficult passage, one thing is clear, Peter is talking about the spiritual baptism that would be carried out by the Holy Spirit. He makes it certain he is not talking about a physical water baptism that simply washes away the physical dirt from the body.

Finally:

Though water baptism is an important symbol of the spiritual Baptism of the Holy Spirit, Paul puts it in perspective when he writes to the Corinthians that he water baptized only two of them, plus one household (I Cor. 1:13-17). He adds that he cannot remember baptizing any others at that church. He concludes the point by adding:

Christ did not send me to baptize, but to preach the gospel, not in cleverness of speech, that the cross of Christ should not be made void (v. 17).

In Ephesians 4:5 the apostle Paul says there is "one Lord, one faith, one baptism." Since the Baptism of the Spirit is a sovereign act of the Holy Spirit whereby all believers are placed into the spiritual Body of Christ, this one baptism would be that Spirit Baptism! Some may miss being water baptized, as may be hinted at by Paul in I Corinthians 1. And, water baptism may be carried out by several methods. But the dynamic, providential work of the Holy Spirit is done to all believers who are then "placed into the body of Christ."

E. The Indwelling Of The Holy Spirit

When a person is born again, the Spirit of the Lord comes within to take up residence. It is this indwelling Spirit that brings about maturity in the life of the child of God.

We begin looking at the issue of indwelling in the New Testament in the book of John. Christ told the Jews that someday they would have rivers of living water within. *"This He spoke of the Spirit, whom those who believed in Him were to receive"* (7:39).

In John 14:17 Jesus told His disciples the Spirit of [related to] truth would come but the world could not receive Him. He told them that right then the Holy Spirit was abiding with them but would someday be within them.

In 14:26 the Lord called the Spirit the (*paraklatos*), the Counselor or "One called alongside." The Father would send the Holy Spirit in Jesus' name. He would teach the disciples "all things" and bring a remembrance to them of everything Christ had related to them.

In 15:26 Jesus told His followers *"I will send to you [the Counselor] from the Father, that is the Spirit of truth, who proceeds from the Father, He will bear witness of Me."* Notice that the Father sends the Spirit and so does the Son! The word "proceeds" could be translated, "continually coming forth from." The task of the Holy Spirit? The verse says, *"He will be witnessing concerning Me."*

Christ points out that the Counselor will not come until He goes away. *"But if I go, I will send Him to you"* (16:7).

The Spirit will share with the believers what God wants Him to impart. He too serves God the Father and He comes to carry out His will. He will communicate all truth and also prophetically tell what is coming:

When He, the Spirit of truth, comes, He will guide you into all the truth; for He will not speak on His own initiative, but whatever He hears, He will speak; and He will disclose to you what is to come (16:13).

The word "guide" is related to the word "road." *"He will steer you into the right road that will lead to all the truth."* Notice verse 15:

All things that the Father has are Mine (v. 15).

The Spirit will disclose all truth. And, the Spirit will disclose what is Christ's and the Father's. What belongs to Him as the Son of God, all these things that are His, also belongs to the Father! The doctrine of the Trinity stands out loud and clear in these verses!

In the Epistles, we will look in more detail at his coming and indwelling of the Holy Spirit in the believer.

CHAPTER 7

HOW THE HOLY SPIRIT WORKS IN BELIEVERS TODAY

The Pauline and General epistles give to us systematically the truths about the Holy Spirit in this Dispensation of Grace or the Church Age. Acts gave us some things that were translated concerning the Spirit of God. But the apostle Paul's first letter, Galatians, was written almost twenty years after Acts 2 and the events at Pentecost. Church Truth, and how the Holy Spirit would operate now, was certainly settled by 49 AD when Paul began writing his letters.

In this chapter we will doctrinally and systematically move through the teachings of the epistles concerning the present work of the Spirit.

A. The Book Of Romans

Rom. 1:4   *[Jesus] who was declared the Son of God with power by the resurrection from the dead, according to the Spirit of holiness.*

Some scholars simply make (*pneuma*) here "spirit." In other words:

77

Christ was raised because of a spirit of holiness!

But many other scholars see this as a direct reference to the Holy Spirit. Part of the reason is that there is a force or power at work that certainly isn't neutral or mindless! The Spirit of God was active in Jesus' coming forth from the grave.

> Rom. 2:29   *But he is a Jew who is one inwardly; and circumcision is that which is of the heart, by the Spirit.*

The Jews generally saw outward circumcision as a sign that they were saved and belonged to God. In this verse Paul tells us true circumcision is not outward but is of the heart. And then he adds: *"by the Spirit of God performs spiritual surgery on new converts."* He removes the pollution of disease prone skin to give new spiritual health!

> Rom. 5:5   *The love of God has been poured out within our hearts through the Holy Spirit who was given to us.*

Since the Spirit has been sent to us as a Counselor, He shares with us how much the Lord cares for and loves us. The Spirit of God tells us that we were once helpless but Christ so loved us, and God the Father so cared, that Jesus died for us the ungodly (5:6).

It is through the Spirit that we really can know spiritual truth and eternal lessons!

> Rom. 7:6   *But now we have been released from the Law, having died to [it] ... so that we serve in newness of the Spirit and not in oldness of the letter.*

In this passage, Paul makes an astounding statement. We died to the Mosaic Law System. Law keeping could never save. In one sense it is still here but we have died to its judgment because we are in Christ. The Law's condemnation He took upon Himself and we "died" with Him. But again remember! Jesus was not dying because of His own sins but because of ours! Law no longer has power over us! We can now serve God through the "newness" of the Holy Spirit. The Greek Lexicon says the word newness (*kainotati*), has the idea of that which is "extraordinary." The work of the Spirit is totally unique!

Also, the Greek word "oldness" can be translated "obsoleteness." The

Law is worn out and we have a new, extraordinary relationship with God's Spirit.

Since Paul wrote the letter to the Galatians before he wrote the Roman epistle, he had asked earlier:

> *Did you receive the Spirit by the words of the Law, or by hearing with faith? Having begun by the Spirit, are you now being matured by the flesh (3:2-3)?*

The answers are of course no! The Law does nothing but judge us.

The Chapter Of The Spirit: Romans 8

Romans 8:1-39 has been called the chapter of the Spirit! There are right at 23 references in this passage referring to Him. We say right at because some verses may simply be referring to the human spirit. (Scholars disagree on a few.)

(Note also that the best Greek manuscripts do not include 8:1b, which reads in older texts: *"who do not walk according to the flesh, but according to the Spirit."*)

Paul's point in this chapter is the empowerment of the Holy Spirit in living the Christian life. In the various verses He says:

1. *For the [principle] of the Spirit of life in Christ Jesus has set you free from the [principle] of sin and death (8:2).*

2. *[We] do not walk according to the flesh, but according to the Spirit (8:4).*

3. *For those who are according to the flesh set their minds on the things of the flesh, but those who are according to the Spirit, the things of the Spirit (8:5).*

4. *Paul will tell us that the believer positionally is no longer living by the principle of the mind of the flesh (8:9). On this basis he adds: For the mind set on the flesh is death, but the mind set on the Spirit is life and peace (8:6).*

5. *You [believers] are not positionally in the flesh but in the Spirit (Greek:*

since) indeed the Spirit of God dwells in you. But if anyone does not have the Spirit of Christ who indwells you (8:11).

6. *The Spirit of Him who raised Jesus from the dead dwells in you. He ... will also give life to your mortal bodies through His Spirit who indwells you* (8:11).

7. *If by the Spirit you are putting to death the deeds of the body, you will live* (8:13).

8. *All who are being led by the Spirit of God, these are the sons of God* (8:14).

9. *You have not received a bondage-spirit leading to fear again, but you have received the Spirit of adoption as sons by which we cry out, 'Abba! Father!'* (8:15).

10. *The Spirit Himself bears witness with our spirit that we are children of God* (8:16).

11. We have the first fruits of the Spirit (8:23). "*The Holy Spirit, the great Giver, having given us this great gift [salvation], we may look on it as the first-fruit of all that He will do for us, including even the redemption of our body from the grave.*" (Bullinger)

12. *The Spirit helps our infirmities; for we do not know how to pray as we should, but the Spirit Himself pleads for us with sighs too painful for words* (8:26).

13. *[God] who examines the hearts knows what the mind of the Spirit is, because He [the Spirit] appeals for the saints according to the will of God* (8:27).

This section is so rich as to what the Holy Spirit does on our behalf. Without Him and His work within, we would be most miserable children of God in this world!

The Spirit And Paul's Conscience

Rom. 9:1   *I am telling the truth in Christ, I am not lying, my conscience bearing me witness in the Holy Spirit.*

Even the great apostle Paul needed confirmation by the Holy Spirit. He realized the Spirit of God was essential to let him know when his thoughts were on target. He writes in regard to his "unceasing" grief, concerning the lost state of his kinsmen the Jews. He tells us it is the Spirit that bears witness with his conscience about this matter. He even wished he could be accursed from Christ if his own people would come to the Lord. The pain Paul was feeling was real. The Holy Spirit confirmed this: "I am not lying, my conscience bearing me witness [concerning my fellow Jews!]"

Frederic Godet notes:

> *"It seems as if Paul wished to confirm his affirmation by a double testimony, that of his conscience and that of the Holy Spirit."*[38]

Everett Harrison as well adds:

> *[Paul's] soul is burdened over [the Jews'] condition, as were the prophets of old. Since he has left Judaism behind, this sorrow might be interpreted as somewhat less than sincere. Hence the solemn introduction in which he summons two witnesses - his union with Christ who is the truth ... and his conscience as aided by the Holy Spirit.*[39]

The Holy Spirit And Kingdom Principles

Rom. 14:17 *For the kingdom of God is not eating and drinking, but righteousness and peace and joy with the Holy Spirit.*

The spiritual essence of the coming earthly Kingdom is important to Paul. The Kingdom will not be simply materialism that pampers the flesh and the appetite. Though the 1,000-year reign of Christ on earth is historical and literal, a spiritual dynamic is at work within the citizens of that Kingdom. We are someday destined to be there in that blessed moment when our Savior reigns and rules. The principles of the Kingdom are in us now "with" the Holy Spirit: righteousness, peace and joy.

Harrison again notes:

> *Mention of the Spirit is understandable [in this passage], because joy and peace are included in the fruit [the Spirit] produces in the believer's life. The list in Galatians 5:22 is not intended to be complete, so*

we may legitimately claim practical righteousness as affected by [the Spirit's] indwelling ... The manifestation of the fruit of the Spirit is acceptable not only to God who provides it, but also to men who see it in operation and experience its blessings.[40]

The Spirit Gives Us Hope

Rom. 15:13   *Now may the God of hope fill you with all joy and peace in believing, that you may abound in hope by the power of the Holy Spirit.*

When the Bible speaks of "hope," the idea is actually "anticipation." We are to anticipate someday being with our Savior. Paul wishes for the believer that they *"may abound in [anticipation] because of the power of the Holy Spirit."* The Greek word "abound" can be translated "to be made wealthy." *"To be made wealthy with anticipation."* Or, *"looking for the Lord's return."* Looking to go home!

Paul Was "Sanctified" To The Ministry By The Spirit

Rom. 15:16   *that my offering of the Gentiles might become acceptable, sanctified by the Holy Spirit.*

In this passage Paul mentions the fact that he is called as a minister of Christ to the Gentiles. He says he is like a priest, ministering the gospel of God. He pictures himself offering up the Gentiles that they may become acceptable, *"sanctified by the Holy Spirit."* The word "sanctified" means "to be made unique, special." Those he is winning to Christ, Paul trusts that the Spirit of God would make them unique in the service of the Lord!

Paul Speaking The Gospel By The Power Of The Holy Spirit

Rom. 15:19   *In the power of signs and wonders, in the power of the Spirit; so that from Jerusalem and round about as far as Illyricum I have fully preached the gospel of Christ.*

Paul reminds the Romans that, when the Gospel went forth from Jerusalem, it went as far as Illyricum, which would be to the Eastern shore of the Adriatic Sea, or to present-day Yugoslavia. It went, he adds, through means of signs and wonders *"by the power of the Spirit."* The Holy Spirit was the Mover of the Gospel by dramatic and miraculous means!

Godet further explains:

> It seems to me more natural to understand: "the (divine) power breaking forth in signs." ... the power of the Spirit [may read] "the power with which the Spirit fills me."[41]

Love That Comes From The Spirit

Rom. 15:30 *Now I urge you, brothers, by our Lord Jesus Christ and by the love of the Spirit, to strive together with me in your prayers to God for me.*

Paul urges the Roman Christians to strive in prayer with him, so that he might be delivered from those who oppose him in Judea and Jerusalem (v. 31). He urges them to do this by the name of *"our Lord Jesus Christ"* and by the love of the Spirit. Most believe the passage better reads, *"the love that comes from the Spirit."* Because of this shared love, the believers should join Paul in his petition to God to be delivered from his enemies.

Harrison throws further light:

> *"By the love of the Spirit." This could mean the love for one another that the Spirit inspires in believers ... But since the phrase is coupled apparently equally with that of the person of Christ, it is probably better to understand it as the love that the Spirit has ... The warmth of the expression is enough to warn us against thinking of the Spirit rather impersonally as signifying the power of God. Paul had already affirmed thee Spirit's deity and equality with Father and Son (II Cor. 13.14).* [42]

B. The Book Of I Corinthians

The church at Corinth had tremendous spiritual problems - jealousies, factions, open sins, and drunkenness. The list goes on and on! In the letter to this group of Christians, Paul had a lot to say about the Holy Spirit and His work.

Demonstration Of The Spirit

I Cor. 2:4 *And my message and my preaching were not in persuasive words of wisdom, but in demonstration of the Spirit and of power.*

As Paul communicated the Gospel, he did so with personal *"weakness, fear and much trembling"* (v. 3). His message was not with persuasive *"words of wisdom"* but with power and demonstration [or proof] by the Holy Spirit. Again, the Mover of the message is the Spirit of God. He is orchestrating the movement of the truth of the Gospel. He is applying it to the hearts of those who are to believe. Paul says the result is, *"your faith should not rest on the wisdom of men, but on the power of God"* (v. 5). Note: *the power of the Spirit; the power of God.*

The Spirit Reveals Spiritual Things

I Cor. 2:10-16   *For to us God revealed [spirit truth] through the Spirit; for the Spirit searches all things, even the depths of God. ... the thoughts of God no one knows except the Spirit of God. ... We have received, not the spirit of the world, but the Spirit who is from God ... we speak not in words taught by human wisdom, but in those taught by the Spirit ... a natural man does not accept the things of the Spirit of God; for they are foolishness to him.*

To believers in Christ, the Spirit of God reveals, illumines "all things, even the depths of God." The word "reveal" is (*apokaluptw*), "to show that which is hidden." The Greek word "illumines," "searches" is (*ereunw*). It is better translated "examines, investigates, explores, traces out, sheds light on," or illumines!

To us, God revealed [all things] through the Spirit; for the Spirit is illuminating all things, that is, the depths of God (v. 10).

Paul adds in v. 11, *"the thoughts of God no one knows except the Spirit of God."* Verse 12 tells us we have received the Spirit *"who is from God,"* through whom we know the things freely given to us by God. This is how we learn spiritual truth and develop that personal relationship with God Himself. The Spirit is the Initiator of this process.

Now we don't have to simply speak words of human wisdom. But we can teach the thoughts of the Holy Spirit (v. 13). As well, the Spirit becomes an Explainer or Interpreter. Verse 13 reads: *"We speak ... by those [words] taught by the Spirit, explaining, interpreting spiritual things to spiritual men."*

(Bullinger) What is it to be a spiritual man? The apostle Paul will explain in the verses that follow.

But first, Paul says in verse 14 that *"a natural [soulish, pseuxikos] man does not receive the things of the Spirit of God; because they are moronic [stupid] to him, and he is not able to understand them, because [those things of the Spirit] are understandable spiritually."*

In Paul's context here, the soulish man is the unsaved person who has not received Christ as Savior. He operates his life totally by his inner self, his own soul.

The apostle goes on and argues:

> *But he who is spiritual understands [examines, investigates] all things, yet he himself no [unsaved] can fully understand* (v. 15).

Paul is saying that the world cannot figure out the person who is spiritual. The lost do not have the Spirit of God who gives comprehension and thus, the non-Christian does not understand the believer who is in touch with the Holy Spirit!

To be spiritual (*pneumatikos*), Paul argues, is to have the Spirit and to be listening to Him; attempting to follow what He says. Paul explains this point in verse 16:

> *For who has known the mind of the Lord, that he should instruct [the Lord]? But we have the mind of Christ.*

Note: 1) The Spirit aids us in knowing the thoughts of God (v. 12). 2) We are taught by the Spirit (v. 13). 3) We have the mind of Christ (v. 16).

Again, how do we have the mind of Christ, and how can we understand the deep things of God?

Because we have the Holy Spirit of God within!

This would have to imply the believer in Christ gets the Holy Spirit at the time of belief. There is no delay in receiving the Spirit of God. He comes within at the Baptism of the Spirit to do all the work described in the letters of Paul and Peter sent to the churches.

The word spiritual (*pneumatikos*) is used almost exclusively by Paul in his letters. It generally means: 1) To be led by the Spirit, 2) or, In reference to other issues that imply "godliness," or that which is instigated by the Spirit.

The Carnal Christian

I Cor. 3:14   *I could not speak to you as to spiritual men, but as to carnal men, as to babes in Christ. ... for you are still fleshly [carnal] For ... there is jealousy and strife among you.*

What is a carnal Christian? The word carnal means "fleshly" [*sarkikos*], and implies the believer can stop listening to the Spirit and live his own way only by what he can touch, see and hear. Thus, living the life by the outward senses rather than by what God says.

Paul tells the Corinthians he could not speak to them as those who would be listening to the Spirit of God (spiritual) but he had to address them as fleshly, because there was jealousy and strife among them (v. 3). Paul says he had to teach the Corinthians with "milk" because they could not take in strong meat. On this, Charles Hodge well remarks:

The same truth in one form is milk, in another form strong meat. "Christ,"" says Calvin, "is milk for babes, and strong meat for men." Every doctrine that can be taught to theologians is taught to children. We teach a child that God is a Spirit, everywhere present and knowing all things; and he understands it. We tell him that Christ is God and man in two distinct natures and one person forever. This to the child is milk, but it contains food for angels. The truth expressed in these propositions may be expanded indefinitely, and furnish nourishment for the highest intellects to eternity. The difference between milk and strong meat, according to this view, is simply the difference between the more or less perfect development of the things taught.[43]

Paul adds that the believers' lives in the church in Corinth was such a mess that they were looking like the world: *"Are you not walking like mere men?"* (vs. 3, 4).

The Holy Spirit is ever with the believer in Christ but He may he grieved and quenched by carnality and sin (Eph. 4:30; I Thess. 5:19). More on this later.

The Church, The Temple Of The Holy Spirit

I Corinthians 3:16-17 and 6: 19-20.

I Cor. 3:16-Il: *Do you not know that you are a temple of God, and that the Spirit of God dwells in you?*

I Cor. 6:19-20:   *Do you not know that your body is a temple of the Holy*

*Spirit who is in you, whom you have from God, and that
you are not your own?*

The apostle Paul refers to the church collectively as a temple of the
Lord, even a temple of the Holy Spirit. Many miss the impact of this passage. Paul uses the plural you, *"all of you (together) are a temple of God, and,
the Spirit of God dwells in all of you together."* Note again the Trinitarian formula: *A temple of God! The Holy Spirit dwells within!*

Paul then says if anyone is destroying the Church, the collective temple of God, the Lord will in the future destroy him (3:17). Though the
Church will face persecution and trials, God will still spare the Church collectively until He takes it home to be with Himself! The language of chapter 3 is different than chapter 6. In chapter 3, all believers are seen as a collective temple for the Spirit of God. In chapter 6, Paul seems to be saying
each believer's "body" is an actual dwelling place for the Spirit. God should
be glorified in our own personal body! "The immoral man sins against his
own body" (v. 20). Hodge aptly writes:

*A temple is a house in which God dwells; and therefore, it is added,
"and that the Spirit of God dwelleth in you." This indwelling of the
Spirit constitutes each believer, every separate church, and the Church
collectively the temple of God. As in the Jewish temple, in its inmost
recess, the Shechinah, or glory of God, was constantly present, and
conferred on the building its awe-inspiring power, and rendered any
profanation of it a direct offence to God; so does the Holy Spirit dwell
in the Church, the profanation of which by false doctrine is therefore
sacrilege.[44]*

The Spirit In The Salvation Process

I Cor. 6:11   *But you were washed, but you sanctified, but you were justified in the name of the Lord Jesus Christ, and in the [working]
of the Spirit of our God.*

It is the Spirit who accomplishes all of these aspects of our salvation.
The Spirit washes [baptizes], "sets us aside" and "legally acquits" us. All of
this makes us children of God! W. Harold Mare adds:

In describing their conversion, the apostle lists three transactions
that occurred at the time when the Lord saved them: they were

washed (*apolousasthe*), that is, they were spiritually cleansed by God, an act symbolized by baptism (cf. Matt. 28:19); they were sanctified (*hegiasthete*), an expression either to be interpreted as an amplification of the concept "washed" (cf. Titus 3:5, 6) or meaning that they had been set apart as God's people (cf. I Pet. 2.9); and they were justified (*edikaiothete*), showing God's act as judge in declaring the sinner righteous because of Christ (Rom. 3:23-26; 5:1).[45]

Paul's Opinion, The Spirit's Directive

I Cor. 7:40   *But in my opinion she is happier if she remains as she is; and I think that I also have the Spirit of God [concerning this matter].*

In 7:25 - 40 the apostle Paul gives instructions concerning distressing times coming on the church and raises the question whether young women should marry, under those circumstances. Though not overly dogmatic, he argues that it is better to remain single because of the "present distress" (v. 26).

At the first of this section, Paul argues, *"I give an opinion"* and *"I think then that this [opinion] is good in view of the present distress"* (vs. 25-26). But at the end he adds, *"but I think that I also have the Spirit of God [behind this opinion]"* (v. 40).

The apostle knew when he spoke authoritatively and when he was offering opinion. Though he felt here that what he was saying was by observation and opinion, he discerned also that the Spirit of God was with what he said.

"Jesus Is Lord!"

I Cor. 12:3   *No one can say, 'Jesus is Lord,' except by means of the Holy Spirit.*

This passage and Gal. 4:6 makes it clear that we receive the Holy Spirit at the point of belief for salvation.

It is impossible then for a young Christian not to have the Spirit. He could not claim Jesus Christ as Master because the words would stick in his throat, without the work of God's Spirit! In like fashion, having the Holy Spirit within, no one could cry out "Jesus is accursed!" (3a).

[The rest of I Corinthians 12 and chapters 13-14, are handled in

Chapter 8, entitled The Baptism (Washing) Of The Holy Spirit And The Giving Of The Gifts]

C. The Book Of II Corinthians

II Corinthians is a follow-up to I Corinthians. Some of the issues in the first letter had not been resolved. (Though some things had been corrected.) In this letter Paul works hard to repeat and explain some things in more detail but also, to defend his apostleship.

II Cor. 1:22 *[God] who also sealed us and gave us the Spirit in our hearts as a pledge.*

In verse 21, Paul argues that his position as apostle was "established" (confirmed, made reliable), and with the Corinthian believers, they were all united with Christ. He says too they were "anointed" in God. This refers to an imparting of knowledge of spiritual truth and knowledge that gives a framework for living the Christian life. The apostle John speaks of this anointing:

You have an anointing from the Holy One, and you all know [spiritual truth] (I Jn. 2:20).

John then also adds: *"This anointing teaches you about all things, and is true"* (2:27).

Paul then says to the Corinthians, God *"also sealed us and gave us the Spirit in our hearts as a pledge"* (1:22).

The apostle repeats this in his Ephesian letter: *"Having also believed, you were sealed in Him with the Holy Spirit of promise, Who is given as a pledge of our inheritance, with a view to the redemption of God's own possession, to the praise of His glory."* (1:13-14).

A seal represented an official declaration in regard to a government administrative decision. Seals are even used today to verify and guarantee the validity of a matter. A biblical example is Daniel 6. When Daniel was thrown to the lions, no one, not even the king could rescue the prophet. 6:17 tells us, *"And the king sealed [the den] with his own signet ring and with the signet rings of his nobles, so that nothing might be changed in regard to Daniel!"*

Nothing can change concerning our salvation. The Holy Spirit is a seal over believers until we are taken home, until the final redemption of God's own possession! Our salvation is not assured by our goodness or self-effort. Salvation for God's children is assured by the Holy Spirit as the seal!

The Spirit of God is our Pledge as well that we have a glorious inheritance waiting for us in glory. The Greek word for Pledge can be translated "first installment, the down payment." The Spirit Himself is our surety! His divine and holy reputation is at stake in regard to our final redemption.

Author Of Salvation, The Spirit

II Cor. 3:3   *The Holy Spirit is the pen that authors salvation in human hearts. Paul writes, You are clearly declared to be the letter of Christ ... written not with ink, but with the Spirit of the living God, not on tablets of stone, but on tablets of human hearts.*

The Corinthians conversion was due, not to human power or wisdom, but to invisible power and grace (Acts 6:3, 5, 8, 10), and to the power and operation of the living God Himself. (Bullinger) The ink and tablets of stone bring reminders of the Old Testament Law that was limited, hard, and unbreakable! But that Law could never bring salvation. Only the Lord and His Spirit can affect eternal life!

Paul continues this argument about the Holy Spirit through 3:18. Again comparing the Law of Moses, Paul says the letter of the Law kills "but the Spirit gives life" (v. 6). He adds that we are now servants of the New Covenant that is initiated by, "of or from the Spirit."

Paul reminds the Corinthians that when Moses came down from Sinai, after receiving the Law from the Lord, his face was filled with glory, which radiance in time faded away (v. 7). Then the apostle adds, *"the ministry of the Spirit [upon us],"* is more glorious than the old order of the Law! The reason is, the Holy Spirit is working in us righteousness and salvation and not condemnation, as does the Law (v. 9). The Law kills, but the Spirit gives life!

The Lord Is The Spirit

II Cor. 3:17-18   A profound passage: Jesus, *"the Lord is the Spirit!"* Paul then adds, *"where the Spirit of the Master [Lord, kurios] is, there is freedom."* By this Paul means freedom from the judgment of the Law.

The apostle then tells us that there is a progressive glorification taking place with us (v. 18). We only see the glory of Christ as if we are seeing His reflection in a brass mirror. *"Beholding as in a [brass] mirror the glory of the Master."* By degree, and as time takes its toll, we are being transformed (metamorphosized) into the identical likeness, "with ongoing glory." Paul then tells us who is accomplishing this: *"it is as from the Master, [even as well] the Spirit!"* It can be emphatically stated that Jesus, along with the Holy Spirit is carrying us to glory.

Faith, A Gift Of The Spirit

II Cor. 4:13   *But having the same spiritual [gift] of faith, according to what is written, "I believed, therefore I spoke," we also believe, therefore we also speak;*

We've already seen that faith is a gift of the Holy Spirit (I Cor. 12:8-9). In that passage, however, I believe Paul is referring to a special gift granted believers. There are those who have this extra dose of trust, the ability to believe when outward confirmations of what God is doing may be lacking.

But in this passage (4:13), I believe Paul is speaking about "saving faith." Some English texts read: *"But having the same spirit of faith"* But from Greek the passage better reads, from what is called a Genitive of Apposition: *"We having the same spiritual gift of faith."* Remember, each time "spiritual" is mentioned; the source is the Spirit of God. In this verse, Paul quotes Psalm 116:10: *"I believed, therefore I spoke."* Paul is using this Old Testament verse to reinforce the idea of a gift given! The apostle then adds: *"We also believe, therefore also we speak."* Or, we were saved, thus we responded. I believe verse 14 that follows supports this view. It is a Saving Faith verse:

Knowing that He who raised the Lord Jesus will raise us also with Jesus and will present us [together] with you.

The Spirit As A Pledge Gives Courage

II Cor. 5:5   *Now He who prepared us for this very purpose is God, who gave to us the Spirit as a pledge.*

How do we really know we'll be with the Lord when we die? This assurance comes through the comfort of the indwelling Holy Spirit. Paul starts his argument in verse 4 when he tells us that our mortal body we are clothed with will someday be swallowed up by the new life in Christ because, God *"prepared us for this very purpose"* (v. 5). He then adds what he said back in 1:22: *God has given to us the Spirit as a Pledge.*

The results: *Being always of good courage, and knowing that while we are at home in the body we are absent from the Lord; for we walk by faith, not by sight, I prefer rather to be absent from the body and to be at home with the Lord.*

This is that great New Testament promise that tells us we go straight home to be with Jesus when we die. There is no delay, no intervening stop at a purgatory! When we expire, we are at home with Christ. This is not so of the lost. They are eternally separated from God and must stand at the Great White Throne Judgment at which Christ will judge them for their works. And all who stand before Him at that final hour, are cast into "the lake of fire" (Rev. 20:11-15).

Walking Through Persecution With The Holy Spirit

II Cor. 6:6   *... in purity, in knowledge, in patience, in kindness, in the Holy Spirit, in genuine love.*

In this context, 6:1-10, Paul tells us that Christians can expect a world of woe and trouble! And yet we're servants of God. We can be assured of *"afflictions, hardships, distresses, beatings, imprisonments, tumults, labors, sleeplessness, hunger, dishonor, evil report, etc."*

In all of this, Paul adds but *"with the Holy Spirit"* (v. 6).

All believers in Christ go through trials and difficulties. We have no guarantees for tomorrow. We do not know what we may have to face. What Paul is saying flies in the face of the Faith Movement that always promises deliverance or prosperity. We do not know how the Lord may use us but we are assured we'll have the comfort and presence of His Holy Spirit!

Believers "Share" The Holy Spirit

II Cor. 13:14 *The grace of the Lord Jesus Christ, and the love of God, and the sharing with the Holy Spirit, be with you all.*

As the apostle closes this letter, he gives to us this astounding greeting by which he mentions all members of the godhead, the Trinity!

Christians experience the fellowship of each person in the Triune God. May each *"Be with you all."*

1.   The grace *from* the Master Jesus Christ

2.   The love *from* God

3.   The sharing *from* the Holy Spirit

This "sharing" is (*koinonia*), "fellowship." It is the Spirit that helps believers to relate and walk about in a common spiritual, mental and emotional bond. And even with His work within all of us, there can develop doctrinal and carnal divisions because, often we are not studying and living in the truth. The Holy Spirit vitally illumines truth but Christians can "quench" His work and "grieve" Him by sin in the life (Eph. 4:30; 1 Thess. 5:19).

D. The Book Of Galatians

About sixteen times in this first letter of Paul (written around 49 AD), the apostle mentions the indwelling of the Spirit and the practical results of this work. In Galatians, Paul is countering Legalism and the Judaizers, i.e. those who say you can trust Christ as Savior but you must also keep the Law for salvation and for Christian living. The apostle comes out blasting this false teaching! He sends this letter to churches in the Greek region known as Galatia. Paul writes in angry tones and shows his disappointment that they are not living fully by the power of the Spirit. He is frustrated that they have taken on contradictory elements of Judaism and are now trying to keep the Law to please God.

Paul argues that only by living our life with the Holy Spirit can we please the Lord!

How Do We Get The Spirit?

Gal. 3:1-5   *... did you receive the Spirit by the works of the Law, ... Having begun by the Spirit, are you now perfected by the flesh? ... Does He who provides you with the Spirit ... do it by the works of the Law...?*

In this paragraph, Paul asks his readers how they got the Spirit of God anyway! *"Did you receive the Spirit by the works of Law-keeping or by hearing with faith?"* The question creates its own answer: *"Through faith and not Law-keeping!"*

Then, Paul asks the Christians in Galatia: *"Having begun by the Spirit, are you now being perfected [matured, completed in the spiritual walk] by means of the flesh?"*

No matter what a believer does, he cannot improve on the gifts of God. The apostle argues that when the Lord began working to save the people in the region of Galatia, He provided miracles and His Spirit in the redemption process.

Were the Galatians earning salvation by Law-keeping and self-effort? Or, was God simply looking for their trust and faith? Paul answers the questions by reverse comment: *"The Holy Spirit comes through our hearing the truth and then applying our sincere belief to His Word"* (v. 5).

The Promise Made By The Holy Spirit

Gal. 3:10-29   This economy or Dispensation of Grace was hinted at in Genesis 12:3: *Through you, Abraham, I will bless all families of the earth.*

Paul refers to this Abrahamic Covenant and the promise of blessing on the Gentiles. Besides some future promise, how was Abraham "saved?" How did he become the Lord's? By Law-keeping? Or, by simply believing what God said? i.e., by trusting what God promised!

The Scripture, foreseeing that God would justify the Gentiles by faith, proclaimed the gospel before to Abraham, saying, 'All the nations shall be blessed in you.' So then those who are of the faith [process] are blessed with Abraham the believer (3:8-9).

As we have seen earlier, this promise ultimately included the giving of the Lord's Spirit. The rest of Galatians brings this out and sees this fulfilled:

1.   *In Christ Jesus the blessing of Abraham [came] to the Gentiles, so that we might receive the promise of the Spirit through faith* (3:14).

2.   *Because you are sons, God has sent forth the Spirit of His Son into our hearts, crying, 'Abba! Father!'* (4:6).

3.   *We through the Spirit, by faith, are waiting for the anticipated [coming]*

of righteousness (5:5). This verse better reads: *We through the Spirit's [gift of] faith, are waiting.*

4. Paul in 5:16-18 tells us the benefits of the Spirit's indwelling and working within us. The apostle will tell us that now we will experience a conflict between the flesh [the desires of the physical] and the Holy Spirit.

5. *I say, be walking with the Spirit, and you will not bring to maturity the craving [greed] of the flesh [physical]. Because the physical sets its desire against the Spirit, and the Spirit against the physical; for these are in opposition to one another, so that you can't do the things that you wish to* (5:16-17).

6. Finally, Paul adds: *if you are led by the Spirit, you are not under the Law* (5:18).

The Fruit Of The Spirit

Gal. 5:22-25   *"But the fruit of the Spirit is love, joy, peace, patience, kindness, goodness, faithfulness, gentleness, self control; ... If we live by the Spirit, let us also walk by the Spirit."*

"But the fruit of the Spirit is..." Some have tried to say that, since the word fruit is singular, the Spirit will thus produce all the spiritual qualities listed in verses 22-23, in each believer, at all times. This is not true. Fruit can be a collective noun but it does not imply that it is "either all or nothing." Below are the nine qualities and fruits that the Spirit is progressively working in us. All of us must admit, we often resist and harden ourselves to some of these important characteristics. So none of us will have coming forth all these Fruit(s)! The Spirit is working within us, but we fail to see our own spiritual resistance to His activity. But here is what we could potentially have from the Spirit of God:

1. Love (*agapa*). In-depth love, having to do with relationships and deeply caring.

2. Joy (*xara*). Related to the words grace (*xaris*) and "to gift" (*xarismatos*). True joy comes from outside of ourselves; it is "graciously

gifted" to us from the Holy Spirit!

3.   Peace (*eirana*). Related to the Hebrew word (*shalom*), with the idea of "emotional stability."

4.   Patience (*makrothumia*). Literally, "to suffer long," "to put up with a lot," or, "to be able to pace oneself in trials."

5.   Kindness (*xrastotas*). Or, generosity.

6.   Goodness (*agathwsuna*). One who is characterized by being and doing good to others.

7.   Faithfulness (*pistis*). One who is characterized by stability and trustworthiness.

8.   Gentleness (*prautas*). Unassuming, considerate, humble, courtesy.

9.   Self-control - Discipline.

Paul then says that there is no rule (or law) against these characteristics. No one can object to these things (v. 23b). He then closes this paragraph by drawing from important principles:

Since we are living (positionally before God) by means of the [work of] the Spirit, let us also be walking (experientially before others) by means of the [work of] the Spirit (v. 25).

Being "Spiritual" When A Brother Falls

Gal. 6:1 *Brothers, even if a man is caught in any trespass, you who are spiritual, restore such a one in an attitude of consideration, each one looking to yourself, lest you too be tempted.*

What happens when a Christian falls into sin? Paul addresses this in this verse. Often, when a believer takes a nosedive morally, other Christians take him out and execute the one who is their own! But it is Paul who argues for restoration. The assumption in the verse is that the fallen brother can turn back to the Lord. Then the "spiritually mature" should "be putting him back in order, be restoring" because the mature brother too may sin someday and need restoration and mercy. The key is the word "spiritual." This implies one who is listening to, following after, trying to be obedient to the Holy Spirit! It does not mean one who is superior before God or one who is better than his brother.

By the way, being "spiritual" is not absolute. There is no perfect Christian. Everyone has his own set of flaws and failures. No brother in Christ can lord it over another Christian.

Sowing To The Physical And Sowing To The Spirit

Gal. 6:8 ... *the one who sows to his own flesh shall from the flesh reap corruption, but the one who sows to the Spirit shall from the Spirit reap eternal life.*

As the old axiom goes, "you reap what you sow." This biblical truth that comes from verse 7 warns that there are consequences in behavior. In 6:8 Paul explains further this truth.

Sowing to the flesh does not reap eternal damnation. But it does reap a rotten life! Our sins may cause us to smell! Sowing to the Spirit may not bring tangible evidence in this life. Believers do much for God that will only be counted in eternity. Sometimes what we do for Him is not seen on this earth. But someday, because of the Spirit, we will see crops that exemplify eternal life in glory!

E. The Book Of Ephesians

This is one of Paul's most powerful books. The great theme of this letter is God's eternal purpose to establish and complete His body, the Church that belongs to Christ. The apostle begins by dealing with the Lord's sovereign choosing, and predestination *"according to His purpose who works all things after the counsel of His will ... that we should be to the praise of His glory"* (1:11-12). Paul goes on and describes the work of the Spirit of God in unusual ways and with unique descriptions.

The Seal And "Down Payment" - The Holy Spirit

Eph. 1:13-14 *Sealed with [Christ] by the promised Holy Spirit, who is our final installment with a view to the "release" of God's own possession to the praise of His glory.*

As we have seen before, Paul adds the "sealing" work of the Holy Spirit and the fact that the Spirit is also our "pledge" or first installment, (down payment), toward our final and ultimate redemption when we are taken home to glory.

A New Access To The Father - The Holy Spirit

Eph. 2:18   *Through [Christ] we both [Jew and Gentile] have our access in one Spirit to the Father.*

In 2:11-22, Paul argues that both Jew and Gentile now can come to the Father "through the Spirit." He says both groups are made "into one [body]." Both are reconciled to God through Christ. God has created a new household built on a new foundation of the apostles and prophets, "*in whom you also are being built together into a dwelling of God because of the Spirit*" (v. 22).

This new household is the Church. As a whole, the nation of Israel, as a whole, as a nation, is outside the place of blessing. The Jews as a people are judicially blinded. But individual Jews join Gentiles in forming this new body. Israel will again someday be brought back into favor, after the Church has been taken home by the Rapture.

The Holy Spirit Reveals And Strengthens The Church

Eph. 3:5, 16   *[The mystery of Christ] has now been revealed to His holy apostles and prophets by the Spirit: that He would grant you, ... to be strengthened with power through His Spirit in the inner man;*

In 3:1-21, Paul continues his discussion of this new entity the Church. He calls it a "mystery," or something not before revealed. The Church is a new Dispensation (*oikonomia*), called in some texts a "stewardship" (3:2) or "administration" (3:9). Paul argues, the Church:

in other generations was not made known to the sons of men, as it has now been revealed to His holy apostles and prophets by the Spirit (v. 5).

Having been placed into the spiritual Body of Christ (by the Holy Spirit) believers can now draw strength from the Lord, because of the ongoing work of the Spirit.

[That the Father] ... would grant you, according to the riches of His glory, to be strengthened with ability by means of His Spirit in the inner [person] (v. 16).

There Is One Spirit, One Master, One God And Father

Eph. 4:3-6   *... being diligent to preserve the unity of the Spirit in the bond of peace. There is one body and one Spirit.*

Because of human weakness, the Church has never experienced perfect unity. Paul pleads for this unity with the Spirit, with the fetters, chains of peace (that should bind believers together) (v. 3). To accomplish this, the apostle sees believers living their relational Christian life "worthy of their calling" (v. 1):

with all humility and gentleness, with patience, showing forbearance to one another in love (v. 2).

Paul wants believers to walk in the same unity seen in the Godhead. To illustrate this, he gives an incredible passage that amplifies the doctrine of the Trinity (vs. 4-6):

There is one [spiritual] body [of Christ] and one Spirit ... one Lord [Jesus], ... one God and Father of all who is over all and through all and in all!

Believers Can Grieve The Holy Spirit Who Indwells Forever

Eph. 4:30   *Do not grieve the Holy Spirit of God, by whom you were sealed for the day of redemption.*

The Doctrine of Eternal Security is clear from this passage. By this, the apostle recognized the Spirit is with us forever. And since He is right with us when we fail, our sins are "felt" by the Spirit who lives within us. The most offensive sins to Him are described in the two verses that follow (vs. 30-32). By our clamor, bitterness, bitterness and malice toward other believers, we bring grief to the Holy Spirit experiences. This fact demonstrates that the Spirit is not simply an inanimate force. He is a person, and personality who emotionally can be joyful or saddened! *"It is not by defects in our general walk as Christians; but in our special failure in not manifesting the kindness, and meekness, and tenderness, and forbearance, which are requisite for the preservation of the spiritual unity of the One Body."* (Bullinger)

The Filling Work Of The Holy Spirit

Eph. 5:18-19 *Do not get drunk with wine, for that is dissipation, but be filled with the Spirit.*

This is the only description of the Filling of the Spirit in all the epistles. As pointed out in Acts, this Ephesian 5 description of Filling is different than what is taking place in Acts. There, it is a sovereign work of God. The word Filling (Greek, *plarow*) normally has the idea of "to be complete, whole, mature." With this in mind, and in light of the context of this passage, I believe the idea is "to control." Three things can be said about this Filling:

1) It is in the Imperative or Command Mood. *"You be controlled by the Holy Spirit."*

2) It is in the Present Tense. *"You be continually, daily controlled, by the Holy Spirit."*

3) It is in the Passive Voice, whereby the action comes back on to the subject. *"You continually [allow] the Holy Spirit to come upon and control you."*

Paul then adds the thought that a process takes place, or results follow that are practical to Christian living. These things take place when the Holy Spirit is in control of the believer's life.

Note the present participles:

1. *Speaking to one another in psalms, hymns, spiritual songs ... (v. 19).*

2. *Singing, making melody with your heart to the Lord (v. 19).*

3. *Always giving thanks for all things in the name of our Lord Jesus Christ to God, even the Father (v. 20).*

4. *And be committing [attaching] to one another with fear regarding Christ (v. 21).*

Standing Defensively Against The Evil Powers

Eph. 6:10-18 *And take ... the sword of the Spirit, which is the Word of God.*

One of the most misquoted passages in Paul's epistles is the so-called "Spiritual Warfare" section of Ephesians 6. Looking carefully at what the apostles says, he is not defining offensive combat but a defensive posture for believers in Christ. How audacious to think that we can ourselves defeat Satan and his forces! But many Christians are in a power play and feel that they have this awesome authority, innately and personally within, to "bind" and control demons and the darkness. They lie to themselves!

The "binding" passages often quoted have to do with authority given the apostles, as they launched the Church. This does not have to do with such "apostolic" authority given now, in this Dispensation, to the average Christian.

We have all heard from those who desperately crave power say, *"I have the gift for spiritual warfare. I can cast out devils and bind and loose."* How silly but also, how anti-biblical! Though indeed Christians do have power, it is not the flamboyant kind that is explosive and makes waves! But again, this passage in Ephesians 6 is defensive in nature. Note Paul's wording:

1. *Put on the armor to stand* (v. 11).

2. *Put on the armor to resist in the evil day, having done all, stand firm* (v. 13).

3. *Stand firm* (v. 14).

4. *Taking the shield of faith to extinguish the flaming arrows* (v. 16).

5. *Be on the alert* (v. 18).

When we "move" at all with God's armor, the feet are to be shod with the "readiness" of the Gospel [that brings] peace (v. 15). And the sword of the Spirit is for fighting off satanic attacks. It is the Word of God (v. 17). By saying the Scriptures (collectively as the Word), *is* what the Holy Spirit uses against evil, i.e., by the truth of the Bible, is telling us this is what we must wield when standing our ground against the darkness. We share and give forth the Word of God. The Holy Spirit dispels the darkness, convicts and converts. Bullinger adds, the Word of God is *"the sword which He, the Spirit, has provided and uses Himself, and which He has given to us for our use."*

Then Paul adds in verse 18, we pray at all times *with* or *by the help* of the Spirit. The Holy Spirit is involved in this prayer process and "petition for all the saints." The Spirit is the source and power of all prayer. (Bullinger)

F. The Book Of Philippians

Philippians is one of Paul's Prison Epistles (61 AD). He knows his life is at stake and that his time is short.

The apostle's relationship with the church at Philippi was always close and cordial. Having helped him financially at least two times before this letter was written, and having heard of his confinement in Rome, the church sent Epaphroditus with another gift. Philippians is a thank you letter. (Ryrie) In it he speaks of the Holy Spirit but not as much as in some other letters.

The Holy Spirit As Support

> Phil. 1:19 *I know that this shall turn out for my deliverance through your prayers and the provision of the Spirit of Jesus Christ.*

In chapter one, Paul says by imprisonment or release, the Gospel will be proclaimed. He adds his great statement of trust, *"For to me, to live is Christ, and to die is gain"* (1:21). Humanly speaking, Paul would like to be set free. He writes that if this happens, *"I know that this shall turn out for my deliverance through your prayers and the provision of the Spirit of Jesus Christ."* (1:19).

The Greek word "provision" is the word used to describe muscles that hold the body together. If he is delivered, the Spirit is that support system that will encourage the apostle. Note he says the Spirit "that belongs to Jesus Christ," or "the Spirit that is from Jesus Christ." Both phrases are almost identical in meaning.

The Sharing In The Spirit

> Phil. 2:1 *If therefore there is any encouragement with Christ, if there is any consolation of love, if their is any "sharing" with the Spirit, if any affection and compassion, make by joy complete by being of the same mentality* (vs. 1-2a).

In the first part of this chapter, the apostle commends the Philippians for their companionship. He says the Spirit of God is the center point around which fellowship [sharing] among believers takes place.

The Holy Spirit is the glue that binds believers together. He activates mutual love and compassion and purpose. It would be a cold Christian experience indeed without the working of God's Spirit within us!

The Spirit Aids Our Worship

Phil. 3:3 *... for we are the true circumcision, who worship in the Spirit of God and glory in Christ Jesus and put no confidence in the flesh.*

Paul starts this chapter warning the church at Philippi of the Judaizers who would love to put Christians back under the Law and the ceremony of circumcision. He warns them of the "false" circumcision, the outward, by which the Judaizers believe they gain spiritual merit with God. Paul then says that they have the "true" circumcision, i.e., those who worship *with* the Spirit of God *"and glory in Christ Jesus and put no rest [conviction, confidence] in the [outward] flesh."*

We believers in Christ do not realize how limited we are, apart from the ongoing work of the Holy Spirit! Paul has said He helps us with our prayers and now the apostle tells us He assists in our worship!

G. The Book Of Colossians

Colossians, like Ephesians, Philippians and Philemon, is a prison letter. Here too, the church was fighting Judaism and other heresies. This letter is very similar to Ephesians. Paul mentions the Spirit but once in this book.

The Spirit Aids Us With Love

Col. 1:8   *[Epaphras] also informed us of your love in the Spirit.*

Paul commends the Colossian church. He speaks of their faith and the love they had with all the saints. He adds that *"the Word of truth, the gospel ... constantly is bearing fruit and increasing in them"* (vs. 5-6).

Paul had sent his assistant Epaphras to the Colossae believers. He returned to Paul and *"informed us of your love [which is] with the Spirit"* (1:8). Just as the Spirit activated worship and fellowship (as mentioned in Philippi), He prompts love between Christians. Remember, Christ promised the Holy Spirit would be our Counselor. He would encourage and bind believers together.

H. The Books Of I & II Thessalonians

The Gospel exploded in the European port city of Thessalonica. Opposition quickly arose from the Jewish and Gentile communities. The church there underwent terrible persecution. In these two letters (51 AD), the apostle Paul continues his inspired description of how the Holy Spirit works in saving believers and then how He continues His ministry within the soul of Christ's own.

I Thess. 1:5-6   *For our gospel did not come to you in word only, but also in power and in the Holy Spirit and with full conviction; ... having received the word in much tribulation with the joy of the Holy Spirit.*

In 1:4 Paul describes the Doctrine of Divine Election: "*Brothers beloved of God, experiencing His choice [out calling] of you.*" He then says the Gospel came to them in more than simply by words but "with power" and "with the Holy Spirit" (v. 5). And, be adds, "with full conviction" or "having completely clothed you."

The apostle goes on and says that the Word of truth came to them in the midst of much tribulation but with the joy from the Holy Spirit (v. 6). The Spirit gave calmness and peace though a religious storm was pouring persecution down upon this new little church.

The Holy Spirit Given To Us

I Thess. 4:8   *He who rejects this [message] is not rejecting man but the God who gives His Holy Spirit to you.*

Paul reminds the believers in verse 7 they are not called of God for the purpose of impurity, but to be *special, unique* (sanctified). We should live godly lives lest we be rejecting "the God who gives His Holy Spirit to you" (4:8). It is a reminder that the Spirit is always with us and we grieve Him by living an impure life (Eph. 4:30).

Do Not Quench The Holy Spirit

I Thess. 5:19   *Do not quench the Spirit.*

Paul continues this theme about holy living in this passage. He urges, "*Do not quench the Spirit [as if putting out a fire]*" Believers can do this by careless living and by ignoring the work of the Spirit within.

The Restraining Work Of The Holy Spirit

II Thess. 2:6-9   *And you know what restrains [the man of lawlessness] now, so that in his time he may be revealed. For the mystery of lawlessness is already at work; only He who now restrains will do so until He is taken out of the way. And then that lawless one will be revealed whom the Lord will slay with the breath of His mouth and bring an end by the appearance of His coming; that is the one whose coming is in accord with the activity of Satan, with all power and signs and false wonders.*

The apostle Paul begins this section by describing the coming apostasy, *"the departure,"* or *"the falling away"* (2:3). Most explain this as the great spiritual decline of true faith in Christ at the close of the Dispensation of the Church. Paul warns the Thessalonian believers not to be deceived. In other words, *"this departure has not come up on the world yet. Don't panic!"*

In fact, by the context, they thought they were already into *"the Day of the Lord"* (2:2) which technically is the seven year prophesied Tribulation period! But Paul says when that horrible period comes *"the man of lawlessness"* or *"the son of destruction"* will have come (2:3b). His evil characteristics are exposed in 2:4. (1) He exalts himself. (2) He takes his seat in the restored Temple in Jerusalem. (3) He portrays himself as God. Almost all agree that this *lawlessness one* is the antichrist who is revealed in the Tribulation and who is the servant of Satan.

Unger writes:

> *Cast out of heaven upon the earth, Satan will operate through the antichrist, that mysterious and ominous personage predicted both in the Old and the New Testaments to arise in the last times.*[46]

Some argue that the antichrist is simply a force or evil power or even Satan as put forth by some. But Chafer rightly argues:

> The claim that this Person [the antichrist] is Satan is as untenable, since Satan cannot be said to restrain himself That the Restrainer is accomplishing a stupendous, supernatural task classes Him at once as one of the Godhead Three; and since the Holy Spirit is the

active agency of the Trinity in the world throughout this age, it is a well established conclusion that the Restrainer is the Holy Spirit of God.[47]

Therefore. Paul argues that the antichrist is restrained or prevented from appearing now! But what or who is keeping him from coming or holding him back? As already mentioned, the Spirit of God Himself!

2:7 says:

"He now restrains ... until he is taken out of the way."
One argument for the "he" is that this is the righteous witness of the Church which restrains the antichrist. But the word for church is (*ekklasia*) which is neuter in Greek and not masculine! And the "he" in the text is actually a masculine pronoun.

The most common rule about the Holy Spirit is that, when speaking of His person (even though *pneuma* is neuter as a word), the masculine pronoun is used. Thus, *"He the Holy Spirit."*

Paul then must be telling us the Spirit of God is the Restrainer, preventing this evil worker of Satan, the antichrist, from coming forth upon the earth until the Tribulation. However, it must be noted that the *"spirit"* of the antichrist is already here (I John 4:3). This is the spirit *"that does not confess Jesus is from God"* (4:3), and is called *"the spirit of error"* (4:6). Many believe John is speaking about a demon that will drive the antichrist and inspire him to deceive the culture and speak lies. That demon is already here, or we should say the power behind him is already in the world. But again, the antichrist is not here yet. He comes at the beginning of the Tribulation.

In II Thessalonians, 2 Paul concludes by telling us that the antichrist will have *"all power and signs and false wonders"* (2:9). He will use the *"trickery"* of wickedness (2:10) and fool all who do not receive the love of the truth, as to be saved (2:10b). God will judge those who following the antichrist. The Lord will send a deluding influence so that they believe what is false (2:11).

The Bible Knowledge Commentary (New Testament) gives a convincing summary on this entire important passage:

Who or what is restraining the satanically empowered movement against God's law and is postponing the revelation of the man of sin?

Some say it is the Roman Empire. But the empire has long vanished and "the holder back" is not yet revealed. Another suggestion is that this is Satan, but it is difficult to see why he would hold back sin. Others suggest that human governments are holding back sin and the revealing of the antichrist. But human governments will not end prior to the antichrist's unveiling. Nor do all governments restrain sin: many encourage it! The Holy Spirit of God is the only Person with sufficient (supernatural) power to do this restraining. (p. 719)

Chosen To Salvation By Means Of The Spirit

11 Thess. 2:13   *We should always give thanks to God for you, brothers beloved by the Lord, because God has chosen you from the beginning for salvation through sanctification by the Spirit and faith in the truth.*

In salvation, the choosing and calling come even before saving faith. Faith is a gift and the result of the Spirit's work (Eph. 2:8-10). A dead man cannot save himself A person blinded by Satan cannot "unblind" himself. Something eternal (and may we say internal) must first happen.

This passage tells us the order of salvation:

God has chosen you from the beginning for salvation through (by means of) sanctification by means of the Spirit and by means of faith in the truth.

The choosing came first. The work of the Spirit and faith were but the instruments. The choosing or calling took place before the foundation of the earth (Eph. 1:4).

I. The Books Of I & II Timothy, Titus
These are Paul's Pastoral Letters, written over a period of about 4 years (A.D. 63-66). Paul continues with the same truths about the work of the Holy Spirit.

Christ Proclaimed Righteous By The Holy Spirit

I Tim. 3:16   *Great is the mystery of godliness [of Christ]: He who was*

> *revealed in the physical, was proclaimed righteous by the*
> *Spirit, observed by angels, proclaimed among the nations,*
> *trusted on by the world, and taken up into glory.*

In this amazing verse, the apostle Paul gives a short, all encompassing anthem, dedicated to the person of Jesus Christ. He sees Jesus' coming as the fulfillment of the revelation of a mystery hidden from earthly view in the past.

In the verse, Paul sees the Spirit as having "vindicated" or "justified" Christ. He was given a stamp of approval by His person and His sacrificial life! Bullinger probably correctly states that ultimately, the Lord is "justified" by demonstration of His resurrection. The resurrection proves Christ totally righteous and perfect and holy. Therefore, the grave cannot hold Him. The dynamic work of the Holy Spirit on the Son, the proclamation of Christ's righteousness, is like a stamp of approval.

The Spirit Prophesies Things To Come

I Tim. 4:1   *But the Spirit is expressly saying (ongoing and right now) that*
             in later times some will fall away from the faith!

Only a few times does the biblical text use the word "says" when referring to the inspiration of the Bible by the work of the Holy Spirit. But this passage says just that.

This passage tells us that the "inspiring" work of God's Spirit is a "speaking." What the Scriptures tell us is what the Spirit is speaking! The two are the same! Thus, we can trust the Word as the speaking of the Holy Spirit. Notice too the Spirit is prophesying the future: He will be speaking about later times.

In 4:1-3, the Holy Spirit prophesies the end of the Dispensation of the Church. Paul says, *"the Spirit emphatically [expressly] is saying that 'in later times some will fall away from the faith.'"* This will be part of the great Apostasy that will close the Church Age.

Even Christians want to be optimistic about the future. But the Holy Spirit gives us the truth. The Church Age will end with a *"Falling away from the faith."*

The Holy Spirit And The New Birth

Titus 3:5   *He saved us, not on the basis of deeds which we have done in righteousness, but according to His mercy, by the washing of regeneration and renewing by the Holy Spirit.*

Beginning with John 3, the New Testament really expounds the concept of the New Birth. It has to do with the Spirit's "washing" and the bringing to life, i.e., to new spiritual life those who are lost. This is salvation itself, all activated by God's Holy Spirit.

In the Titus 3:5 passage, Paul makes it clear we're not saved by works of righteousness. We're saved by the process of the bath (*loutron*) of the again-birth (*palm* = again, *genesia* = birth), or re-creation. (Bullinger) The next word in the text is and (*kai*) and possibly could read: "*by the bath of the again-birth that is, even the again-making of the Holy Spirit.*"

The word *again making* is (*ana* = up), again, (*kainwsis* = newing), or, remaking (making anew) of the Holy Spirit. This reminds us clearly of the words of Christ, "*You must be born again*" (Jn. 3:7).

Here the word of salvation is described as having been the work of God; and it is declared to be not the work of man by his own good works, but the act of God: "He saved up."[48]

J. The Book Of Hebrews

The book of Hebrews was written to convince the nation of Israel that Jesus was their Messiah. Though handed over to certain Christians mentioned at the end of the book, the epistle was really a preamble or declaration of independence for the nation of the Jews, in regard to the deity of Christ, and His great sacrifice for them.

The Holy Spirit is mentioned a lot in the book and this tells us that the Jews had a sophisticated view of Pneumatology and the work of God's Spirit. Ryrie notes: "*All evidence points to the [readers'] Jewish background — thus the title of the book, 'to the Hebrews.'*"

Another Mention Of "The Gifts Of The Spirit"

Heb. 2:4   *God also bearing witness ... by signs, wonders and ... by various miracles and by gifts of the Holy Spirit according to His will.*

The writer of Hebrews must have known the apostle Paul because this verse reads like I Corinthians 12:4 and 11. In this 2:4 passage, the author of Hebrews (whose name is unknown) mentions the signs and miracles performed as a witness to the nation of the Jews and, he adds the evidence of the "*gifts of the Holy Spirit.*" In other words, the list of gifts in I Corinthians

12 were mainly for convicting Israel about salvation and the truth of their own Savior.

The Holy Spirit And Inspiration

Heb. 3:7   *Therefore, just as the Holy Spirit says, "Today if you hear His voice."*

This verse reminds the Jews that the Old Testament is the speaking of the Holy Spirit. The passage quoted is a kind of paraphrase of Psalm 95:8. The psalm itself is a call to the people to praise the Lord. It has a human composer but, according to the writer of Hebrews, the ultimate author is the Holy Spirit Himself!

Therefore, just as the Holy Spirit says.

Here, it is the Holy Spirit, as the direct Inspirer of Scripture, speaking through "holy men of God" (II Peter 1:21).

Hebrews 10:15-17 says the same things: *"The Holy Spirit also bears witness to us, for after saying, ... He [the Spirit] then says."* The writer then quotes Jeremiah 3 1:33-34!

What is written, the Holy Spirit is saying.

The Curse Upon Israel

Heb 6:4-6   *... been made partakers of the Holy Spirit, and have tasted the good word of God ... and then have fallen away, it is impossible to renew them again to repentance.*

This passage is probably one of the most misunderstood sections of the Word of God.

These verses are used to argue loss of believer salvation. They have been used to deny Eternal Security. The reason? They have been directly applied to believers in Christ. Most see the verses aimed at those who proclaim Jesus as Savior, and then fall away and lose their salvation!

But a careful analysis, beginning with the whole book of Hebrews, and then this specific passage, shows that this section is a warning to the Jews who but "tasted" salvation when Christ was ministering to the nation. The writer uses words that speak only of being "enlightened." In other words, his descriptions in verses 1-5 do not really describe receiving Jesus the Messiah as Savior! The passage is referring to the fact that the nation of Israel saw the "evidence" that Christ was their king, and they then reject-ed Him!

Regarding the Holy Spirit, the author writes that some of his Jewish audience may have only been "partakers" of His work. The word partaker (*metoxos*) is used to describe those who together witness a sports event or see the same play together. But the word does not imply the strong concept of being acted upon by the Spirit so as to be "born again!"

The nation of Israel partook "with" the Holy Spirit in that He was the "witnesser" to the nation of Christ and His ministry. It does not imply they were acted upon by God's Spirit to the point of salvation. In other words, the Jews had all the evidence, all the testimony. They saw Jesus' deeds and miracles. And after having all that evidence. If they still walked away from the Lord:

it would be impossible to renew them again to repentance (6:6).

Bullinger well notes concerning the Jews in this section of Hebrews:

Nothing is said about their having received "grace." it is now as it was in the Old Testament Dispensation: (pneuma) may "come upon" persons for service, without being "within" them for salvation. We are not told what they believed; or how much they believed. Whether, as Jews, they believed in Christ as the Messiah of Israel; or whether, as lost sinners, they believed in Christ as the Savior. Hence, these words in Heb. 6 may well have been addressed to such Hebrew believers as they were, [i.e., they had a limited belief about Christ but they did not believe in Christ]. (p. 120)

Thus, once they had rejected personal faith in Him, their rejection was permanent because the Spirit would not come again to witness to the nation of Israel.

The Holy Spirit Speaks Through The Tabernacle

Heb. 9:8   *The Holy Spirit is signifying this, that the way into the holy place has not yet been disclosed, while the outer tabernacle is still standing.*

In Hebrews 9, the author describes the workings of the tabernacle: the place of the shewbread, the altar, lampstand, etc. In verse eight the writer suddenly says: *"The Holy Spirit is signifying this, that the way into the holy place has not yet been disclosed, while the outer tabernacle is still standing."*

In other words, what is written about this sacrificial offering is actually the words and thoughts of the Spirit of God for our learning! This is similar as to what the writer of Hebrews said when he quoted Psalm 95:7 back in 3:7: *"Therefore just as the Holy Spirit says."*

On 9:8 Bullinger writes:

> *Here the statement is that the Holy Spirit in inspiring Moses to write the account of the Tabernacle in Exodus had a meaning beyond what Moses himself understood. It does not say that Moses "signified" anything in what he wrote; but the Holy Spirit "signified" many deep spiritual truths, which He revealed [to the author of Hebrews], and afterwards made known to us.*

The Spirit's Work In The Death Of Jesus

Heb. 9:14   *How much more will the blood of Christ, who through the eternal Spirit offered Himself without blemish to God, cleanse your conscience from dead works to serve the living God?*

Several important things must be noted about this passage. First, the Spirit of God is called "eternal." This is the same "forever" attribute that the Father and Son have. Thus, the Spirit *is* God! For nothing is "eternal" but God Himself!

Second, the Holy Spirit was somehow an agent assisting in the offering of Christ for our sins. This is certainly a mystery that is difficult for us to understand! It was *by means of* the energy of the Holy Spirit that Christ's spotless human nature was formed (Lu. 1.35), and could be *"offered to God"* on our behalf. (Bullinger)

In similar language, the writer of Hebrews speaks of one who tramples under foot the Son of God, by considering unclean the blood of the New Covenant, *"by which [a person] was sanctified, and [thus] has insulted the Spirit of grace"* (10:29) The author in no uncertain terms is telling us that the work of Christ on the cross is orchestrated by God's Spirit. To reject Christ's sacrifice is to reject the wisdom and working of the Holy Spirit.

The Spirit then, made effective, operative and viable the sacrifice of Jesus for sins. Therefore, we can say dogmatically:

1.   By the Father's desire
2.   By the Son's sacrifice
3.   And the working of the Spirit, we now have salvation!

K. The Books Of I & II Peter

Four times in chapter one of I Peter, the apostle mentions the Holy Spirit. Three of these references have to do with Inspiration and the communication of the truth to us. In II Peter, the apostle picks up the same theme in regard to the Inspiration of Scripture and the work of God's Spirit within the prophets.

The Sanctifying Work Of The Spirit

I Pet. 1:2   *[To the scattered strangers] according to the foreknowledge of God the Father, by the sanctifying work of the Spirit, that you may obey Jesus Christ and be sprinkled with His blood.*

The doctrine of Sanctification is taught in this verse. It says we are "sprinkled with [Christ's] blood" and, "sanctified" by the Spirit. Sanctification is in two forms: positional and experiential.

Positional has to do with our being cleansed and "set aside" by the Spirit because we are united to the spiritual body of Christ. The word "sanctify" is (*hagios*) which has to do with being made special, unique or "set aside." Paul speaks of this positional work of the Spirit:

God has chosen you from the beginning for salvation through sanctification by the Spirit and faith in the truth (II Thess. 2:13).

Prophecy And The Work Of The Spirit

1:10-12, and II Peter 1:20-21; these two sections deal with the "inspiring" work of the Holy Spirit in the prophets of the Old Testament:

I Pet. 1:10-12... *prophets who prophesied of the grace that would come to you ... seeking to know what person or time the Spirit of Christ within them was indicating as He predicted the sufferings of Christ and the glories to follow. ... in these things which now*

have been announced to you through those who preached the
gospel to you by the Holy Spirit sent from heaven — things into
which angels long to look.

II Pet. 1:20-21   *... no prophecy of Scripture is a matter of one's own inter-*
pretation, for no prophecy was ever made by an act of
human will, but men moved by the Holy Spirit spoke
from God.

1.   In 1:11, Peter writes about the prophets who longed to know concerning the prediction of the sufferings of Christ and the glory that
would follow. Peter adds they sought to know what person and
what time the Spirit might be indicating. He says (v. 10) they
"carefully investigated," "questioned," and "searched out" these
issues. These prophets of the Old Testament were receiving truth
from the Holy Spirit. They wanted to know more. But the Spirit of
God limited that knowledge. Or, gave it to them by *progressive rev-*
elation, building truth on top of truth.

2.   *And 1:12 adds: it was revealed to them that they were not serving*
themselves, but you, in these things which now they have been
announced to you through those who preached the gospel to you by the
work of the Holy Spirit sent from heaven.

In II Peter 1:20-21, the apostle continues this issue of Inspiration of the
Scriptures. He notes that prophecy did not come through the prophets, in
terms of their own ideas or interpretations (v. 20). Nor did they give forth
prophecy on the basis of their own personal human will (v. 21). But he
states they were men who were:

moved by the guidance from the Holy Spirit (V. 21).

And by this these prophets spoke from God! The Greek preposition
(*hupo*) is placed before the Holy Spirit and before God! Therefore this verse
could read:

Men were moved by the guidance from the Holy Spirit, [they] spoke by
the guidance from God!

There is a parallelism going on in the passage. The Holy Spirit and God
[the Father] are of the same essence! They are the same! Though, they are

different *persons* in the Godhead.

L. The Books Of I John & Jude

There are but few references to the Holy Spirit in these two small books. But what they report of Him is powerful and in some cases relate directly to the Doctrine of the Trinity.

Jesus And The Spirit Dwelling Within

I Jo. 3:24   *And we know by [keeping His commandments] that He abides in us, by the Spirit whom He has given us.*

This verse tells us that Christ abides [remains, stays] within by God's Holy Spirit.

The Spirit is the instrument or conveyer of the Person of Christ right into our very being. The Holy Spirit and Jesus are One in the Godhead. And they have their varied functions. The Spirit works within the believer and as well, the Son will dwell within the believer as He promised. This passage would imply that both Persons were taking up residence inside of us!

False Prophets And Testing The Spirits

1 Jo. 4:1-2   *Do not believe every spirit, but test the spirits to see whether they are from God; because many false prophets have gone out into the world. By this you know the Spirit of God: every spirit that confesses that Jesus Christ has come in the flesh is from God.*

The apostle John cautions believers to beware of lying spirits. By this he could mean false "philosophies" or "beliefs." Or, he could be referring to deceptive demons that manipulate and distort truth. Since he writes of the "spirit" that *"confesses that Jesus Christ has come in the flesh is from God,"* John more than likely is referring to a teaching, a philosophy, or message! Believers are susceptible to misread lies unless they are aware of what is happening about them.

In this paragraph, John gives some guidelines. He warns that the spirit of antichrist is working (v. 3). And, he notes that many false prophets have gone out into the world (culture). He adds, *"every spirit that does not confess Jesus, is not from God"* (v. 3). *"And this is the spirit of the antichrist,*

of which you have heard that it is coming, and now it is already in the world."
But then he previously has noted in v. 2 that the safeguard is the Holy
Spirit!

> By this you know the Spirit of God [because] every spirit that confess-
> es that Jesus Christ has come in the flesh is from God!

In John's day, there was the cult of Gnosticism that taught (among
other things), that Jesus was but a floating spirit, an apparition. It denied the
reality of His physical body. John is here blasting away at this false teaching!

The apostle carries his argument to a conclusion in 4:6. He writes of
the "Spirit of truth." Some translations use the lower case here, and do not
see this as the Spirit of God but simply as "the philosophy of truth," or "the
spirit of truth." I believe it refers to the Holy Spirit. Thus, the verse would
read:

> We are from God; he who knows God listens to us [the apostles], he
> who is not from God does not listen to us. By this we know the Spirit
> of Truth and the spirit [attitude/philosophy] of error.

John still continues all of this same thought along when he writes in
4:13:

> By this we know that we abide in Him and He in us, because He has
> given us of His Spirit.

The Witness Of The Spirit, Water And Blood

I Jo. 5:6-8   It is the Spirit who bears witness, because the Spirit is truth.
                For there are three that bear witness, the Spirit and the water
                and the blood; and the three are in agreement.

The apostle says the Spirit, the water and blood witness to the person
of Jesus Christ. As well, the passage repeats what John has already said
several times, "the Spirit is the truth" (5:7). What does John mean by all of
this?

Most believe the water refers to Jesus' inauguration for His earthly
ministry at the baptism in the Jordan River by John the Baptist (Mk. 1:9-

11). The blood of course refers to our Lord's crucifixion and death on the cross for sins. The greatest witness to Christ is the work of the Spirit. The Spirit confirmed that Jesus was sent from the Father. The Spirit was active in the Lord's ongoing ministry. And, the Spirit dwells within believers giving a testimony and witness to Christ.

Praying By Means Of The Spirit

Jude 19-20   *These are the ones who cause divisions, worldly- minded, devoid of the Spirit. But you, beloved, building yourselves up on your most holy faith; praying in the Holy Spirit.*

Jude has much to say about apostasy and "professors" and not "possessors." He writes against false teachers and lying proclaimers of "religion." He reminds his readers that the apostles warned of "mockers, following after their own ungodly lusts" (v. 18). He argues that they will cause divisions, being worldly-minded and devoid of the Spirit (v. 19).

Jude urges Christians to stay close to the Lord! He argues strongly that we who trust Christ must "keep ourselves in the love of God, waiting anxiously for the mercy of our Lord." Jude reminds us to *"build ourselves up in the faith."* And, to keep *"praying in the Holy Spirit."* What does he mean by this last phrase?

More than likely Jude means to be praying *with* the Spirit or *"praying with the Spirit or with the power from on high."*

M. The Book Of Revelation

The Holy Spirit is mentioned significantly enough in Revelation. He plays a key role when the Church is mentioned. But He is not mentioned as often during the horrors of the Tribulation period, which takes up most of the chapters in the book.

The Seven-Fold Manifestation Of The Holy Spirit

Rev. 1:4 *Grace to you and peace from Him who is and who was and who is to come; and from the seven Spirits who are before His throne.*

The *"who is, was, and is to come,"* most scholars believe is a strong verbal description of God the Father. Mentioning "His throne" would add to that view. Some difference of opinion comes about with the expression "seven Spirits." Many understand this to refer to the Holy Spirit in His perfect fullness since "seven" is the number of completion and perfection. (Ryrie) In similar fashion, it may refer to the seven-fold manifestation of the Spirit of God. This makes sense in light of the seven-fold reference of the Spirit in Isaiah 11:1-2. In this Old Testament passage, the Holy Spirit of the Lord will rest on the Messiah who of course is Jesus Christ. The Spirit will empower Him to serve His Father on earth. The Isaiah passage would read:

A Branch [the Messiah] from [Jesse'] roots will bear fruit. And a Spirit of the Lord will rest over Him, a Spirit of wisdom, understanding, counsel, strength, knowledge, and fear of the Lord.

This appears to be what John in Revelation is referring to. Note in this Revelation 1:4-5 passage, there is a strong hint of the Trinity. John writes:

1. Grace from Him (God the Father)
2. Grace from the seven-fold Spirit
3. Grace from Jesus Christ.

Since the Persons of the Trinity are co-equal, they may all equally impart Divine Grace to believers. This seven-fold manifestation of the Spirit is also repeated by John in 3:1; 4:5; 5:6.

"I Was In The Spirit On The Lord's Day"

Rev. 1:10 *I was in the Spirit on the Lord's Day, and I heard behind me a loud voice.*

As the unfolding of the revelation began, John the apostle tells us he was empowered by the Spirit to receive this incredible message! He writes this here in 1:10 (and also in a similar way in 4:2 and 17:3).

Bullinger rightly notes:

What we are told is that John, by the power and agency of the Holy Spirit was transported into a sphere of heavenly vision, where he saw the future scenes of judgment unveiled, which will one day be a dread reality.

Hearing What The Spirit Says

Rev. 2:7 *He who has an ear, let him hear what the Spirit says to the churches.*

As John addresses the seven churches of Asia in chapters 2-3, he reminds his readers they are reading what the Spirit dictated to the old apostle. Most of these churches were failing spiritually and John gives them sober reminders of judgment. Inspiration of Scripture is again in view as John writes this warning.

The apostle repeats this three more times (2:11, 17, 29) as he warns the churches of their sins and spiritual laxity.

The Spirit Confirming The Voice From Heaven

Rev. 14:13   *I heard a voice from heaven, saying, "Write, 'Blessed are the dead who die in the Lord from now on!'" "Yes," says the Spirit, "that they may rest from their labors, for their deeds follow with them."*

Deep into the Tribulation that is described so vividly in Revelation, there is a description of those martyred who are now seen in heaven. John hears a voice from heaven telling him to write that they are "Blessed," that is, *those who die in the Lord from this point forward!* The Spirit confirms this.

Of course, that blessed rest is with God Himself in heaven!

The Holy Spirit Carries John To See The New Jerusalem

Rev. 21:10   *And [the angel] carried me away in the Spirit to a great and high mountain, and showed me the holy city, Jerusalem, coming down out of heaven from God.*

As Revelation closes, there is the disclosure of The Eternal State and the coming down to the renovated Earth the New Jerusalem. This will be the new center of the universe and the dwelling place of Christ with the redeemed for eternity.

John the apostle is taken on this Divine tour by the Spirit of God:
[An angel] carried me away by the power of the Spirit to a great and

high mountain, and showed me the holy city, Jerusalem, coming down
out of heaven from God.

The Spirit's Call To Accept Salvation

Rev. 22:17   *And the Spirit and the bride (Jerusalem and its inhabitants)*
say, 'Come.' And let the one who is thirsty come; let the one who
wishes take the water of life without cost.

In the last few words of the book of Revelation, there is the personal
appeal to the reader to accept the message of the book, to turn to Jesus as
Savior.

It is the mission of the Holy Spirit then, to invite the long exiled
nations of mankind to again enjoy the beauties and glories of a restored creation, to eat of the tree of life, and to drink of the water of life in the midst
of the Paradise of God!

The Holy Spirit joined with the bride [of Christ], the church, in
extending an invitation to all who heed. Those who hear are encour-
aged to respond and also to extend the invitation to others. The won-
derful promise is given that all those who are thirsty may come and
will receive God's free gift. This is the wonderful invitation extended
to every generation up to the coming of Christ. Those who recognize
their need and realize that Christ is the provider of salvation are
exhorted to come while there is yet time before the judgment falls and
it is too late. As the Scriptures make clear, the gift of eternal life... is
free. It has been paid for by the death of Christ on the cross and is
extended to all who are willing to receive it in simple faith.[49]

THE BAPTISM (WASHING) OF THE HOLY SPIRIT AND THE GIVING OF GIFTS

A charismatic friend of mine (who confesses that his church is not very charismatic) admitted to me he had never taught any of the "charismatic" passages, especially I Corinthians 12-14. This would be like a Baptist pastor never teaching on baptism!

The point I'm making is that often people have never tightly exegeted this important section of God's Word. Thus, there is no wonder there is great confusion on the issues of gifts, tongues and the Baptism of the Holy Spirit.

A. Baptism of the Holy Spirit

It is through the Baptism of the Holy Spirit that we receive the gifts of the Spirit. The Baptism is the washing whereby we are cleansed by God's Spirit. By this, we are placed into the spiritual body of Christ (12:12). We become part of Him. All believers are equal in Christ (12:13). We all drink of "one Spirit" (12:13).

And because of this, gifts are sovereignly given to each believer in Christ!

John Walvoord is correct in this warning:

> *Any view which denies that speaking in tongues used actual languages is difficult to harmonize with the Scriptural concept of a spiritual gift. By its nature, a spiritual gift had reality, and being supernatural, needs no naturalistic explanation.*[50]

And Joseph Dillow concludes:

> [Paul] specifically says that tongues are foreign languages spoken here on earth in I Cor. 14:10, 11. ... It is clear that the languages under discussion here in this chapter are those "in the world." Furthermore, the word-translated foreigner is the Greek word (*barbaros*), one who speaks a foreign language known here on earth. Paul's foregoing comparison between tongues and the sounds of inanimate musical instruments like harps and bugles (I Cor. 14:7-10) merely implies that from whatever source they come, sounds must be distinct and meaningful. Paul is not suggesting that tongues are non-tongues like musical sounds. Rather, the reverse, tongues must be distinctly spoken languages just as a note from a harp or trumpet must be distinct to be effective and meaningful. In the fact of this evidence, we have to conclude that New Testament tongues must have taken the form of meaningful, known words and languages.[51]

B. Gifts Sovereignly Given

Some say you can ask for the spiritual gifts. Many believe in praying for the gift of tongues (languages). But the verses in this section of Scripture will fly in the face of that view. Just the opposite is true. The Spirit gives gifts as He pleases, to whom He pleases!

1. *But to each one is given the "disclosure" of the Spirit for the common good (12:7).*

2. *But one and the same Spirit works all these things, distributing*

(making allotments, appointments) to each one individually just as he wishes (12:11).

3. *God has placed the members, each one of them, in the body [of Christ], just as He desired (12:18).*

In Romans 12:3-8 Paul also discusses the gifts. Here, his list is different then the one in I Corinthians. Though mentioning prophecy and teaching, which are in I Corinthians, he also lists some different ones such as: serving, exhorting, giving, leading and showing mercy.

In Romans as well, Paul mentions the fact that the gifts are sovereignly given. *"We have gifts that differ according to the grace given to us"* (12:6).

C. Not All Have The Same Gifts

Paul makes this clear by saying, *"The body is not one member, but many"* (12:14). He goes on and says that a body has toes, ears, hands and feet. So the body of Christ. *"There are many members, but one body"* (12:20). Each of the body parts are different but all play an important role. He adds: *"You are Christ's body, and individually members of it"* (12:27).

Further:

"All are not apostles, are they? [No] All are not prophets, are they? [No] All are not teachers, are they? [No] ... All do not have gifts of healings, do they? [No] All do not speak with languages, do they? [No]" etc., etc. Paul lists almost all the gifts and makes sure we understand that everyone does not have the same gift.

And in Paul's Romans list he adds: *"All the members [of the body] do not have the same function"* (12:4).

D. Healing, Miracles

When looking at the issue of gifts, an important question needs to be asked. If God sovereignly gives the gifts, must He be giving them all in all periods of Church History? And, could He be giving certain gifts to just certain ones, in distinct time periods, for specific reasons? For example, the gifts of healing and miracles!

There is an interesting conclusion we must come to when thinking about healings and miracles. Healings and miracles are mentioned in I

Corinthians 12:10, 28. When checking these words with a concordance, there is a shocking conclusion one must come to. Only the apostles, Christ, and a few other special apostle-like individuals (such as Stephen) could exercise healing and miracles (powers, Greek *dunamis*). In other words, as far as the New Testament tells us and shows us, *only special people were endowed with these gifts, not the average believer!*

E. Prophecy Was Teaching

One who prophesies speaks to men for edification and exhortation and consolation... one who prophesies edifies the church (14:3-4b).

Though the apostles spoke and wrote far-off prophetic utterances, there was the gift of prophecy given for a specific purpose by the Holy Spirit. And in almost all contexts, it is easy to see that it has to do with teaching rather than "forecasting!" Prophecy was one of the "communicative" gifts whereby the message of the Gospel was moved and spread by special individuals, before the New Testament was completed. The prophets were special "explainers" or teachers to make clear spiritual truth.

We know they were not infallible by what I Corinthians 14 tells us:

1. Prophets had to have confirmation and could only speak by two's and three's (v. 29).

2. By comparing what the prophets said, others in the congregation could "pass judgment" (v. 29).

3. Prophets had to speak in a set order, and one at a time, so there could be learning and exhortation (v. 31).

4. Prophets had to check and balance each other and each other's messages: *"The spirits of prophets are subject to prophets."* (v. 32).

5. If someone is a true prophet, he will not argue with the rules here set down by Paul:

If anyone thinks he is a prophet or spiritual, let him recognize that the things which I write to you are the Lord's commandment. But if anyone does not recognize this, he is not recognized (vs. 37- 38).

F. The Communication Gifts

In I Corinthians 13, Paul mentions what I label "the communication gifts:" prophecy, languages, and knowledge. These three gifts moved the message of the Gospel when there was no completed New Testament canon. 1) The gift of prophecy was given to bring teaching to the Church as to what was doctrinally correct and true. 2) Languages (tongues) were given to move the message of the Gospel from foreign language culture to culture. Apparently, it was used only in a few places in Scripture: Jerusalem and Pentecost, Caesarea and Cornelius' house, Ephesus and Corinth.

In Acts 2, we know that tongues (languages) were dialects and foreign languages. Some try to say that tongues in I Corinthians 12-14 was something different than in Acts 2. But biblically, linguistically and hermeneutically, this view is far from what the plain truth of Scripture teaches.

For example, in Acts 2:4 the passage says they spoke "with other tongues." The Greek is (*heterais glwssais*). A similar technical phrase is used in I Corinthians 14:10: (*heterw gena glwsswn*). By adding the word (*gena*), the phrase would read: "*to another person, [he receives] families (stock, race) of languages*." The one who was gifted by the Spirit could speak miraculously with more than one language.

I Corinthians 13: mentions the gift of knowledge. Apparently, certain ones had special understanding about spiritual issues. They could interpret what was going on and what the Spirit of God was doing in the new fledgling churches. After the New Testament canon was completed, this gift was no longer needed.

These communication gifts of I Corinthians 13 (prophecy, language, knowledge) would someday disappear, Paul says in the Greek text: *Loved will never be falling down, but if there are gifts of prophecy, they will in the future be made inoperative; if there are languages, they will in the future stop themselves; if there is knowledge, it will in the future stop itself* (v. 8).

Paul states here these gifts will cease, but exactly when? Some say only when Jesus "the perfect comes" because "the partial" will then be done away with (v. 10). The problem with this interpretation is that the word perfect is (*to teleion*) and means "the complete, whole, mature." But too, it is in the neuter gender so it could not refer to Jesus who would be in the masculine gender! We can translate the words, "when the completeness comes" or "when the complete thing" should come.

Granted that no one can be dogmatic, yet Paul seems to be referring specifically to these three communication gifts already mentioned. Most educated Greek scholars also believe Paul is referring to the completion of the canon of Revelation. Thus, these special communication helps from the Spirit are not needed today!

If the gift of languages continued after the time of the New Testament, could we see evidence of it in early Church History? One would think so. But this is not the case. In fact, just the opposite is true. The Church fathers tell us the gift of languages used to be around, but they were no longer around in their own period of history. Note, they said "languages" not a gibberish that is unintelligible!

For example, Irenaeus, Chrysostom, Augustine and Eusebius:

Irenaeus (A.D. 120-202) - *The church father Irenaeus wrote, shortly after the New Testament period, these comments on I Corinthians: [Paul] calling these people "mature" who have received the Spirit of God, and who through the Spirit of God do speak in all languages, as he himself also wed to speak. In like manner we do also hear [now of] many brothers in the church, who possess prophetic gifts, and who through the Spirit speak all kinds of languages (Against Heresies, Vol. 1)*

Chrysostom (A.D. 345-407) - *On I Corinthians 12 he writes: This entire passage is very obscure: but the obscurity is produced by our ignorance of the facts referred to and by their cessation, being such as then used to occur but now no longer take place. (Homilies On First Corinthians, Vol. XII.)*

Augustine (A.D. 354-430) - *In the earliest time, "the Holy Spirit fell upon them that believe; and they spoke with tongues," which they had not learned, "as the Spirit gave them utterance." These were signs adapted to the time. For there behooved to be that beckoning of the Holy Spirit in all tongues, to show that the Gospel of God was to run through all tongues over the whole earth. That thing was done for a sign, and it passed away. (Ten Homilies On The First Epistle Of John, Vol. VII.)*

Eusebius - *This church father writes about an ascetic, Montanus (A.D.126-180), whom some label as a demon-possessed heretic: A recent convert, Montanus by name, through his unquenchable desire for leadership, gave the adversary opportunity against him. And he became beside himself and being suddenly in a sort of frenzy and ecstasy, he raved, and began to babble and utter strange things, prophesying in a manner contrary to the constant custom of the Church handed down by tradition from the beginning. Some of those who heard his spurious utterances at that time were indignant, and they rebuked him as one that was possessed, ... And he stirred up besides two women, and filled them with the false spirit, so that they talked wildly and unreasonably and strangely (Church History, Vol. 21)*

G. Desiring The Gifts

In most biblical translations, I Corinthians 12:31 reads something like this:

But earnestly desire the greater gifts. And I show you a still more excellent way.

The Greek word (*zaloute*) is translated "earnestly desire." It could also be translated "be zealous for." But why would Paul tell the Corinthians to be earnestly desiring the greater gifts when he has just told them that not everyone has the same gifts. God gives to each as He pleases, 12:11, 18. Not one gift is more important than another. So again, why would Paul say what most translations report?

Could it be that this passage is mistranslated? It could be! For the verb (*zaloute*) can be translated three ways. This is very unusual for the Greek language, but this happens to be the case with this word. Here are the choices:

"You should strive for the greater gifts." A subjunctive mood.

"Earnestly strive for the greater gifts." As it now is in most English readings. An imperative mood.

But I suggest a third choice is better and more fitting with the overall context of the passage. And "context" is a powerful determining factor in Bible translation! It could read:

"But you are striving for the greater gifts" and implied, you shouldn't be! An indicative mood.

It is my opinion that Paul is actually chiding them because they were not satisfied with the gift they may have had personally. They were making comparisons of each other and this is probably why Paul wrote earlier "there is jealousy and strife among you" (3:3).

Paul is then possibly saying, *"you are out zealously seeking [what you consider] the better gifts. But I will show you a better way to do things. ... if I have not love, I am nothing"* (12:31, 13:3).

H. Rules For Gift Of Languages

What is passed off today as the gift of languages, in all cases, does not fit the rules Paul lays down in I Corinthians 14. In every case observed, there is violation as to what Paul says. Below is a list of those principles:

1. Paul says prophecy, which was a form of teaching, was the better gift above languages (vs. 1-3).

2. The reason: languages were for an outsider who could not understand the language of those in the church. He needed to hear in his own dialect. But the church, by prophecy, could be edified, exhorted and consoled (vs. 2-3).

3. A language speaker edified himself because he was exercising his own gift, but teaching prophecy fed the church, which was better (v. 4).

4. To show off one's gift of language was wrong. If one did speak with this gift, there had to be some valuable spiritual content, not simply talking into the air (v. 6)!

5. The believers at Corinth must have had a pride in the gift of languages. But the average church member sitting in the group could not understand them (because the gift of languages is given to help people visiting in the church who can't understand what is being said. It was for foreigners and strangers!) (v. 12).

6. For those who did not know the language uttered, there had to be interpreters in the congregation (vs. 13-14).

7. The gift of languages was clearly to be exercised audibly. Some miss Paul's point in verses 14-17. He's actually *not* arguing for silent language uttering. He says it must be audible.

8. Paul actually argues for clear teaching over the gift of language, more than likely because the majority in the audience could understand what was being said (vs. 18-19).

9. Paul adds that the way they were abusing languages proved they were childish (v. 20).

10. The gift of languages is actually for unbelievers not for believers. Prophecy or teaching was to be done for believers (v. 22).

11. But if even an unbeliever comes into the assembly who understands the dialect of the group, and suddenly hears a foreign language given by the gift, he will think you are mad. Teaching, overall, is the best thing that should be going on in the church (vs. 23-24).

12. The final and most important rule is that everything should be done to edification (v. 26).

13. And, if language is used, it needs to be confirmed by two or three and then also with an interpreter (vs. 27-28).

The four locations where languages were exercised were melting pots of races, nationalities, dialects and languages. At Corinth the abuse of the gift was great because of the carnality and immaturity of the Christians. Once the Canon of the New Testament was firmed up and completed in writing, the gift apparently faded from use.

Finally, it must be remembered that for anything to be spiritually real and genuine, the Spirit of God must be behind it. And He will not violate the biblical rules laid down in scriptural revelation! If there is anything contrary to this, it is not of God!

CHAPTER 9

FINAL THOUGHTS ON THE WORK OF THE HOLY SPIRIT

A. The Holy Spirit Is Our Guide

Christ and His Spirit cannot be the sufficient guides of an immortal spirit [like ours], unless they have a truly infinite understanding. We have daily inward guidance, by the Holy Spirit and providence applying the Word [of God to our needs]. Christ, through His Holy Spirit, begins His kingly work with us, by "subduing us unto Himself" This is effected in the [Holy Spirit's] work of regeneration. Our sanctification also demands omniscience. For He (the Spirit of God) who would cure the ulcer, must probe it; [because] the heart is deceitful beyond imagination.[52]

B. The Spirit Communicates With Us

We pray to the Spirit for the communication of Himself to us, that He may, according to the promise of our Lord, dwell in us, as we pray to Christ that we may be the objects of His unmerited love. Accordingly

131

*we are exhorted not "to sin against," "not to resist," not "to grieve"
the Holy Spirit. He is represented, therefore, as a person who can be
the object of our actions; whom we may please or offend; with whom
we may have communion, i.e., personal [relationship with]; who can
love and be loved; who can say "thou" to us; and whom we can invoke
in every time of need.*[53]

C. The Same Spirit Works In Us Who Worked In Jesus
*Abraham Kuyper notes: The same Holy Spirit who performed His
work in the conception of our Lord, who attended the unfolding of His
human nature, who brought into activity every gift and power in Him,
who consecrated Him to His office as the Messiah, who qualified Him
for every conflict and temptation, who enabled Him to cast out devils,
was the same Spirit who performed His work in His resurrection, so
that Jesus was justified in the Spirit (I Tim. iii. 16), and who dwells
now in the glorified human nature of the Redeemer in the heavenly
Jerusalem.*[54]

D. The Spirit Carries Out The Work Of God In The World
*In general it may be said that it is the special task of the Holy Spirit
to bring things to completion by acting immediately upon and in the
creatures [of God]. Just as He Himself is the person who completes the
Trinity, so His work is the completion of God's contact with His creatures and the consummation of the work of God in every sphere.*[55]

E. Streams Of Living Water
*The life giving power of the Spirit is brought to a focus in Christ's con-
versation with Nicodemus. "That which is born of the Spirit is spiritual." The life-giving power of the Spirit is vividly set forth in the
account of the conversation between Christ and the woman of
Samaria. "The water which I will give to him will become ... a well of
water springing up for life eternal." The streams of living water flow-
ing forth from the hearts of believers evidently signify the power of the
Holy Spirit in the missionary program for this age.*[56]

F. The Holy Spirit Who Called Us
*Martin Luther wrote: I believe that I can not, by my own reason or
strength, believe in Jesus Christ my Lord, or come to Him: but the
Holy Spirit has called me by His gifts, and sanctified and preserved*

me in the true faith: just as He calls, gathers, enlightens, and sancti-fies the whole Christian Church on earth, and preserves it in union with Jesus Christ in the one true faith; in which ... He daily forgives richly all my sins, and the sins of all believers; and will raise up me and all the dead at the last day, and will grant everlasting life to me and to all who believe in Christ. This is most certainly true.[57]

G. The Holy Spirit As The Giver Of Life

We believe in the Holy Spirit, the Lord, the Giver of life, Who works freely as He will, without Whose quickening grace there is no salva-tion, and Whom the Father never withholds from any ... and we give thanks that He has in every age moved on the hearts of men; that He spake by the prophets; that through our exalted Savior He was sent forth in power to convict the world of sin, to enlighten the minds of men in the knowledge of Christ, and to persuade and enable them to obey the call of the Gospel; and that He abides with the Church, dwelling in every believer as the Spirit of truth, of holiness, and of comfort.[58]

ENDNOTES

1. *Basic Theology*, Charles C. Ryrie
2. Hodge, A.A. *Outlines Of Theology*. Carlisle, Penn.: Banner of Truth, 1991, pp. 173-175.
3. *Circles of Hope*. Maryknoll, NY: Orbis, 1992, p. 30
4. Rowthorn, Anne: *Caring for Creation*. Wilton, CT: Morehouse, 1989, p. 104
5. Chafer, Lewis Sperry. *Systematic Theology, Vol. I*. Dallas: Dallas Seminary Press, 1976., pp. 3, 5.
6. Hodge. A.A. *Outlines Of Theology*. Carlisle. Penn.: Banner of Truth. 1991, pp. 173-174.
7. Enns, Paul. *Moody Handbook Of Theology*. Chicago: Moody, 1989, p. 245.
8. Pink, Arthur. *The Holy Spirit*. Grand Rapids: Baker, 1993, p. 13.
9. Smeaton, George. *The Doctrine Of The Holy Spirit*. Carlisle, Penn.: Banner of Truth. 1988. P. 1.
10. Pache, Rene. *The Person And Work Of The Holy Spirit*. Chicago: Moody, 1979, p. 16.
11. Morris, Henry. *The Genesis Record*. Grand Rapids: Baker, 1993. Pp. 51-52.
12. Morris, Henry. *Ibid.*, pp. 170-171.
13. *Leupold, H.C. Exposition of Genesis*. Columbus, Ohio: Wartburg Press, 1942, p. 255.
14. *Commentary On The Old Testament, Job*. Peabody. MS: Hendrickson, 1989, p. 218.
15. *Ibid.*, p 1032.
16. *Ibid.*, p. 585.
17. Kirkpatrick, A.F. Grand Rapids: Baker, 1982, pp. 612, 612.
18. *Commentary On The Old Testament*, Psalms. *Ibid.* p. 135.
19. *Ibid.*, p. 347.
20. Walvoord. John. *The Holy Spirit*. Wheaton: Van Kampen, 1954, p. 53.
21. Pache. Rene. *The Person And Work Of The Holy Spirit*. Chicago: Moody, 1979, p. 37.
22. Hendriksen, William. *The Gospel Of Luke*. Grand Rapids: Baker, 1981, p. 71.
23. Whitelaw, Thomas. *Commentary On John*. Grand Rapids: Kregel, 1993, p. 35.
24. Thomas, David. *Gospel Of John*. Grand Rapids: Kregel, 1980, p. 37.
25. Walvoord, John. *Prophecy Knowledge Handbook*. Wheaton: Victor, 1990, pp. 184-185.
26. *Commentary On Matthew*. Grand Rapids: Kregel, 1980, p. 61.
27. Walvoord, John. *Jesus Christ Our Lord*. Chicago: Moody, 1969, p. 151.
28. Toussaint, Stanley. *Behold The King*. Portland: Multnomah, 1981, p. 74.
29. Toussaint. *Ibid.*, p. 318.
30. Pentecost, J. Dwight. *Things To Come*. Grand Rapids: Zondervan, nd, p. 123.
31. J.A. Alexander. *Commentary On The Acts*. Grand Rapids: Zondervan, 1956, p. xiv.
32. *The Expositor's Bible Commentary, Acts*. Grand Rapids: Zondervan, 1981, p. 253.
33. *Acts*. Grand Rapids: Baker, 1990, p. 54.

34. *Ibid.*, p. 61
35. *Ibid.*, pp. 77-78.
36. Walvoord, John, Ed. *The Bible Knowledge Commentary, New Testament.* Wheaton: Victor. 1934, p. 373.
37. *The Bible Knowledge Commentary, New Testament.* Ibid., p. 461.
38. *Commentary On Romans.* Grand Rapids: Kregel, 1984. p. 339.
39. *The Expositor's Bible Commentary.* Grand Rapids: Zondervan, 1984, p. 102.
40. *Ibid.*, p. 149.
41. *Ibid.*, p. 480.
42. *Ibid.*, pp. 159-160.
43. *I & II Corinthians.* Carlisle, PA: The Banner of Truth Trust, 1988, p. 49.
44. Hodge. *Ibid.*, p. 59.
45. *The Expositor's Bible Commentary.* Grand Rapids: Zondervan, 1984, p. 223.
46. Unger Merrill F. *Biblical Demonology.* Chicago: Scripture Press, 1955, p. 190
47. Chafer. *Systematic Theology Vol. VI*, p. 86
48. *Word Studies Of The Holy Spirit.* E. W. Bullinger, p. 177
49. Walvoord, John F. *The Bible Knowledge Commentary, New Testament.* Revelation. Wheaton: Victor, 1984, p. 989.
50. *The Holy Spirit.* Grand Rapids: Zondervan, 1978, p. 182.
51. *Speaking In Tongues: Seven Crucial Questions.* Grand Rapids: Zondervan, 1976, p. 22.
52. Dabney, R.L. *Systematic Theology.* St. Louis; Presbyterian Pub., 1978, pp. 200-201.
53. Hodge, Charles. *Systematic Theology, Vol. I.* Grand Rapids; Eerdmans, 1977, p. 525.
54. Thiessen, Henry. *Lectures In Systematic Theology.* Grand Rapids: Eerdmans, 1990, p. 254
55. Berkhof, L. *Systematic Theology.* Grand Rapids: Eerdmans, 1962, p. 98
56. Buswell, James. *Systematic Theology Of The Christian Religion.* Grand Rapids: Zondervan, 1977, pp. 113-114.
57. Luther's *Small Catechism.*
58. *Articles Of The Faith.* Presbyterian Church in England. 1890.

Other books by Mal Couch

Classical Evangelical Hermeneutics
ISBN Prefix #0-8254-2367-8
Pages: 372
Edition: paperback

> Words...grammar...syntax...context — all of these elements form the basis for hermeneutics, the principles and practice of interpreting works of literature. Here is a set of written tools and guidelines for an accurate interpretation and understanding of Scripture. Topics covered include: A history of interpretation and the various hermeneutical traditions in Christian history; An examination of dispensational hermeneutics in the early church; The importance of the doctrine of inerrancy in Bible interpretation; and Understanding symbols and types in biblical prophecy.

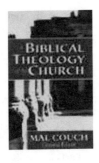

Biblical Theology Of The Church
ISBN Prefix #0-8254-2361-9
Pages: 336
Edition: hardcover

> One of the most popular topics among Christians is how to "do Church." Should it be traditional of contemporary? What should the music be like? Should it target a specific group? Often lost in this discussion are far more crucial and basic questions such as, "What does God intend for the church to be? What does the Bible say about the function and organization of the local church?" A Biblical Theology of the Church takes up the task of defining the mission and function of the local church from a biblical perspective. As noted in the Introduction, "This should be the finest hour for the gospel and for the church of Jesus Christ. At every turn there are urgent opportunities to share the truth in both word and deed. The gospel should be going forth as never before, and believers in Christ should be growing in spiritual maturity. The church should be foundationally solid and a strong bastion proclaiming God's sovereignty and will. Local congregations should be centers of light and places of refuge where comfort and hope is dispensed and renewed."

The Fundamentals For The Twenty-First Century
ISBN Prefix #0-8254-2368-6
Pages: 656
Edition: hardcover

In the early decades of the twentieth century, a prophetic series
of books took a bold stand in the debate over the essential meaning of Christianity. With the publication of The Fundamentals: A
Testimony to the Truth, a new term entered religious language,
fundamentalism, which then meant an adherence to the funda-
mental doctrines of biblical Christianity. Nearly a century later,
biblical Christianity faces similar challenges, both from within
and without its ranks. The term fundamentalism and the faith it
represents have been debased by cultural change, entrenched
secularism, and theological confusion. This new landmark work,
with contributions from thirty-four notable Bible scholars, pastors, and teachers, sets forth a distinctively biblical agenda for the
Christian faith in the twenty-first century.

Issues 2000
ISBN Prefix #0-8254-2363-5
Pages: 160
Edition: paperback

The evangelical faith that produced the historic work, The
Fundamentals, in the early 20th century finds itself, once again,
challenged by cultural change and theological confusion.

A Bible Handbook To The Acts Of The Apostles
ISBN Prefix #0-8254-2360-0
Pages: 464
Edition: hardcover

Numerous evangelical scholars combine their insights to present
an in-depth look at the major doctrinal themes of Acts from a dis-
pensational perspective. It also provides definitions and identifi-
cations of the people, places, and terms used in the Acts of the
Apostles. Includes numerous charts and maps. This book com-
bines the best of a Bible handbook and a biblical theology.

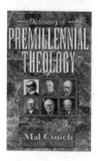

Dictionary Of Premillennial Theology
ISBN Prefix #0-8254-2351-1
Pages: 448
Edition: hardcover

More than fifty scholars combine their expertise to present a historical and topical dictionary of premillennial theology.

Biblical Arts Center

The Biblical Arts center is a museum whose sole purpose is to utilize the arts as a means to help people of all faiths more clearly envision the places, events and people of the Bible. Artworks, ranging from Old Masters to contemporaries, are displayed in both permanent and changing galleries. The Colonnade Gallery, Miracle at Pentecost Gallery and the Founder's Gallery feature works such as "Rebekah at the Well," Madona and Child," and "The Resurrected Christ." Changing every six to eight weeks, the East Gallery features exhibitions ranging from ancient archaeological artifacts to contemporary spiritual art.

The highlight of the Biblical Arts Center is the "Miracle at Pentecost" Mural. Measuring 124 feet wide by 20 feet tall, and featuring more than 200 Biblical characters, many of them life-size, the mural took many hours of Biblical research and over 2 1/2 years to paint. Taken from Acts 2 in the Bible, the mural is artist Torger Thompson's historical interpretation of the day of Pentecost. The painting is unveiled several times a day with a 30 minute light and sound presentation.

The construction of the Biblical Arts Center is distinctly Romanesque, reminiscent of early Christian-era architecture. From the limestone entrance modeled after Paul's gate in Damascus, to the heavy wooden doors, arches and stone columns, the building evokes a strong feeling of Biblical times.

The Center welcomes visitors from across the nation to see the Miracle at Pentecost painting, and the other paintings and sculptures in the museum. You many visit the Biblical Arts Center at:

7500 Park Lane at Boedeker
Dallas, Texas 75225
(214) 691-4661
www.biblicalarts.org